KV-046-068

Language Development in Schools for Children with Severe Learning Difficulties

JOHN HARRIS

LIVERPOOL POLYTECHNIC
I. M. MARSH CAMPUS LIBRARY
BARKHILL ROAD, LIVERPOOL,
L17 6BD 051 724 2321 ext. 216

LIVERPOOL POLYTECHNIC LIBRARY

3 1111 00176 0063

Harris, J
Language development in schools for chil
M M 371.9 HAR 1988

CROOM HELM
London • New York • Sydn

© 1988 John Harris
Croom Helm Ltd, Provident House, Burrell Row,
Beckenham, Kent, BR3 1AT

Croom Helm Australia, 44-50 Waterloo Road,
North Ryde, 2113, New South Wales

Published in the USA by
Croom Helm
in association with Methuen, Inc.
29 West 35th Street
New York, NY 10001

British Library Cataloguing in Publication Data

Harris, John
    Language development in schools for
    children with severe learning difficulties.
    1. Learning disabilities 2. Language arts
    — Remedial teaching
    I. Title
    371.9′044   C4704

    ISBN 0-7099-5702-5
        0-7099-5715-7 (Pbk)

Library of Congress Cataloging-in-Publication Data

ISBN 0-7099-5702-5
    0-7099-5715-7 (Pbk)

Printed and bound in Great Britain by
Biddles Ltd, Guildford and King's Lynn

CONTENTS

Contents

Contents

TABLES AND FIGURES

Tables

Tables and Figures

Tables and Figures

For my father Ron Harris

PREFACE

Spoken language is so much a part of our everyday lives that we can easily take it for granted. It is only when we encounter people who are unable to speak or to understand other people's speech that we are made aware of the enormous range of ordinary everyday activities which depend upon fluent language. Similarly, it is easy to overlook the achievements of children in learning a language and it is only when we ask the question, 'how do children manage to do it?' that we begin to realise the magnitude of the task. Language learning has been described as 'the greatest intellectual feat anyone of us is ever required to perform' (Bloomfield, 1933, p. 29). If this is true, then how much greater must be the challenge to these children who suffer from severe mental handicaps.

Many mentally handicapped children experience considerable difficulties with language learning and require considerable help and encouragement if they are to become confident language users. Many families naturally look to special schools to provide the right kinds of language learning experiences for these children so that they can have a better chance of learning in school and a happier and more fulfilling life outside. This book reports a research study which explores the way in which teachers seek to encourage language development among mentally handicapped pupils in special schools.

It describes the complexity of language both from the point of view of our attempts to understand in detail the range of abilities which together constitute spoken language and in terms of the kinds of experience which seem to be relevant for learning language. It also provides a detailed description of the language assessment and language teaching activities in special schools. Some of the evidence

may be seen as presenting a rather gloomy view of
the child's experiences in school and a critical
picture of the role of teachers. However schools are
but one part of an educational system which together
with the social and health services are designed to
promote the welfare and development of handicapped
persons. The criticisms in this study are therefore
a reflection not so much of teachers as individuals
as the system within which they have to work. In
particular, evidence suggests that teachers in
special schools require far greater support from
other professionals and from researchers if they are
to be able to meet their responsibilities more
effectively. On a more positive note, schools also
present children with many useful and productive
experiences which they would not otherwise have. It
is hoped that this book will help teachers and
others involved with severely mentally handicapped
children to look critically at existing language
learning opportunities in schools and to think
postively about strategies for change.

ACKNOWLEDGEMENTS

I should like to thank the University of Wales who
provided a research grant which made possible the
collection of the data reported in this book and the
local authorities throughout Wales who permitted me
to approach the various special schools. Also, I am
indebted to the many teachers who gave their time
and energy to fill in yet another questionnaire with
nothing but a promise from an anonymous researcher
that the research results would be made available at
some vague future date. I should like to thank the
staff of the Computing Centre at University College
Cardiff who cope so cheerfully with the quirks of
successive versions of SPSS and the researchers who
always find it easier to pick up a phone rather than
the SPSS manual. I am indebted to numerous people
who have, at various times, given generously of
their time and expertise including Dr. Trevor Jones,
Barry Johnson and Dr. Jackie Stedman. Dawn Wimpory
deserves a special 'thank you' for her meticulous
reading of the draft manuscript and her many
detailed and perceptive margin notes. Tim Hardwick
of Croom Helm has been extremely supportive in
helping a rather disjointed research report find the
light of day, and I should like to acknowledge the
valuable comments made by Tim's anonymous reviewer.
The fact that my handwriting is so appallingly bad
is at least part of the reason why I must also thank
two typists who laboured over various parts of the
manuscript, Carol Grant and Nicola Perry. Finally,
thanks to Helen James who is responsible for typing
the Camera Ready Proofs.

In spite of my appreciation for the help and
guidance of friends and colleagues, I claim sole
responsibility for the oversights and limitations
which remain.

Chapter One

INTRODUCTION

This introductory chapter considers some of the
practical issues relating to the educational
provision for mentally handicapped children and the
creation of language learning experiences in
schools. This leads on to a discussion of the aims
of this study. There follows an outline of the
design of the study, the selection of the
participating schools, and a brief account of the
questionnaires which were used to collect the
research data.

PRACTICAL ISSUES RELATING TO LANGUAGE INTERVENTION
IN SPECIAL SCHOOLS

Who are the Children in Special Schools?
In the last ten years there has been much discussion
and considerable legislative progress towards
integrating many children with special educational
needs into ordinary schools. However, it seems
likely that in Britain special education in
segregated schools will continue to be regarded as
desirable for some children. Warnock (1978)
suggested that provision in special schools would
continue to be needed for, among others 'children
with severe or complex physical, sensory or
intellectual disabilities who require special
facilities, teaching methods or expertise that it
would be impractical to provide in ordinary schools'
(page 123;para 8.8). It is precisely because such
schools are regarded as making the best kind of
provision for children with a variety of
disabilities that it is important to try and

understand exactly what the needs of these children might be and to explore ways in which the schools can most effectively meet those needs.

Schools for children with severe learning difficulties are designed to provide an educational environment for those children with primarily intellectual impairments who are unable to benefit from ordinary schools or schools which cater for pupils with moderate learning difficulties. By definition such schools make provision for the least able children including those who suffer from a wide variety of handicapping conditions. For this reason the term <u>mental handicap</u> is often generally applied to the children in such schools although the term 'severe learning difficulties' is now considered more appropriate as a formal description. This term serves to underline the fact that for these children the primary problem is in making sense of their experiences.

All the pupils in these schools have difficulty in making sense of the world around them: this may include their ability to categorise experiences and form abstract concepts, their ability to relate one experience to another, to remember information and to use existing knowledge to solve problems and organise their own behaviour. Some children may be diagnosed as suffering from clearly identifiable conditions, for example, Down's Syndrome, while others may belong to no clearly defined clinical group. Some children may suffer from specific handicaps which contribute towards and exacerbate their low functioning, for example, additional sensory or physical handicaps. However, where such additional handicaps are present, it is assumed that the main developmental and educational difficulties arise from cognitive rather than sensory or physical impairments. In many cases the precise cause of a child's difficulties may be impossible to determine. In this study all the children are referred to as suffering from severe mental handicap and, where appropriate, as having additional more specific handicaps or disorders.

The majority of mentally handicapped children who attend special schools experience considerable difficulties with language (Leeming, Swann, Coupe and Mittler, 1979). In many cases these difficulties arise as a direct result of the more general problems these children have in making sense of and organising their everyday experiences. However, it is likely that some children suffer from more specific linguistic difficulties which are obscured by their generally low level of functioning. In order to avoid making unwarranted assumptions about the cause or causes of the linguistic difficulties evidenced by these children, the terms 'language difficulties' and 'language disorder' will be used to refer to all children whose language is giving cause for concern. It is suggested that the terms language 'delay' and 'deviant language' ought properly to be reserved for conveying rather more precise information about the pattern of abilities and disabilities of individual children (see Chapter Two, pages 15-16).

Language and the Special School Curriculum

One of the ways in which many mentally handicapped children differ from ordinary non-handicapped children is with respect to their command of language at comparable chronological ages. For this reason, the language of mentally handicapped children has received a great deal of attention from both educators and psychologists. Poor language may make it difficult for parents and teachers to communicate with a mentally handicapped child. This may cause frustration for both the child and the adults in the child's life and may make it more difficult for them to establish positive and fulfilling personal relationships with each other.

Inevitably, linguistic difficulties make it more difficult for mentally handicapped children to become independent of adults and to be accepted as individuals within the community. Difficulties with spoken language are also one of the most obvious manifestations of mental handicap for the public at large. It is perhaps natural for mentally handicapped children to be compared with other children and, in social settings where communication is expected, language difficulties emphasise the handicapped child's limitations. On the other hand, improvements in the child's linguistic skills represent an improved ability to cope with the immediate environment, an increased chance of integration within the community and a closer approximation to normal developmental patterns. Language thus represents an important focus for the 'normalising' educative processes of special schools. It is for these reasons that language has been elevated to its pre-eminent position within the special school curriculum (Warnock, 1978, 11:13; Leeming, Swann, Coupe and Mittler, 1979 and Chapter 5 below).

In special schools, as in other schools, language is the principal vehicle for communication between teachers and pupils and is thus central to the process of education. It permits the <u>transmission</u> of the formal curriculum and enables teachers and pupils to construct an additional 'hidden curriculum' concerning <u>inter alia</u> ground rules for organised social interaction and a set of values for evaluating both formalised knowledge and personal conduct (Mercer and Edwards, 1981; Romaine, 1984). However, in special schools language has a third important role; it is also treated as a <u>subject</u> within the curriculum and special schools have come to see the task of encouraging language development as one of their major responsibilities. The inclusion of language development as a subject for teaching raises numerous important issues. On one hand language development is increasingly being recognised as a cognitive and social process which arises, at least partly, as a result of a child's experience of social interactions with other people. On the other hand, traditional views on effective teaching, together with the influence of behavioural psychology, has created a rather different classroom ideology for the special school. This approach emphasises specific teaching objectives, the decomposition of complex skills into simpler more easily learned units and formal instructional methods in which the teacher controls the content, direction and pace of the lesson (Warnock, 1978, 11:5). Within this setting, language has come to be regarded as something which can be analysed, made an object of public scrutiny and taught alongside a wider curriculum of subjects. Above all it suggests that the best way of assisting children to learn language is to assimilate language to the traditions and practices of the classroom. It might be predicted that the contradictions inherent in these two approaches to encouraging language development would surface within the special school.

This analysis thus gives rise to a number of questions which are of theoretical interest and also have profound implications for practice. For example, what kinds of classroom experience are regarded as being relevant to the acquisition of language? What conceptual tools do teachers bring to bear on the task of creating optimal language environments? Should language be regarded as a skill which can be decomposed into its constituent sub-skills and taught systematically or is language best thought of as a developmental phenomenon which requires a different approach to other subjects? How far do teachers take account of developmental theories in planning learning experiences? Are some forms of classroom experience more beneficial in terms of language learning than others? These and similar questions provided the impetus for this study and it is hoped that answers to some of them will be provided in this book.

The Need for Systematic Intervention

Language is often regarded as a natural product of human development; as non-handicapped children grow older, so they become more proficient in their command of language. In so far as most normal children do develop language without apparent effort and without the need for deliberate teaching, this intuitive account is reasonably accurate. However, this explanation of language acquisition has not satisfied many linguists and developmental psychologists who have sought a more detailed explanation of the course of language development and an understanding of the factors which influence it. Whereas research on language development is undertaken because of scientific curiosity about a natural phenomenon, the case of mentally handicapped children who have associated language disorders raises different issues. For these children language development does not always follow the same pattern or proceed at the same pace as the language of ordinary non-handicapped children.

The question then becomes whether or not it is possible to provide special forms of experience for mentally handicapped children so that they can be more successful in language acquisition. What precisely is meant by 'more successful' will be dealt with more fully in the next chapter. At this point it need only be mentioned that success can be defined in two ways: success might be measured by how well the child is able to respond to everyday situations in which he/she might be called upon to use language. Alternatively, success might be defined in terms of how similar the mentally handicapped child's language is to the language of ordinary non-handicapped children of a similar age. The former definition calls for a detailed description of the communicative demands of everyday situations, while the second definition calls for a detailed description of the course of 'normal' language development. The relationship between these two ways of assessing language will be dealt with more fully in Chapter Two.

The idea of providing special forms of experience to assist language development derives from the view that language is at least partially influenced by the particular experiences which any child is exposed to. For example, children grow up to speak different languages or dialects, or to speak with particular accents depending upon the language they hear around them. Research on non-handicapped children has also demonstrated that, in many ways, both what is learned and the speed of language acquisition are related to specific experiences. It is argued that if a mentally handicapped child experiences difficulties with learning, and in particular with certain areas of learning concerned with language acquisition, then it ought to be possible to organise these language related experiences to compensate for the child's difficulties and thus facilitate more effective language acquisition. Given this premise, the central question for those concerned with language intervention for mentally handicapped children becomes, what experiences will be most beneficial for different children? Unfortunately, this question turns out to have a rather complicated answer which requires a consideration of contemporary research on language development.

If adults are to be effective in providing supports for more effective language acquisition then it is necessary to establish both a detailed framework for describing language at different stages of development, and a theory which explains how language develops. This might be summarised as the 'what' and the 'how' of language development. With an understanding of what patterns of behaviour are included under the heading of 'language' a teacher may be able to assess language development more accurately and thus identify areas of a child's linguistic performance which need special support. With a model of 'how' language develops teachers will be in a better position to determine what kinds of support are appropriate to enable individual children to make optimal progress.

Thus the problem of how to provide the most effective learning opportunities for mentally handicapped children can be expressed in terms of assessment and planned intervention. Assessment is necessary to determine the pattern of a child's abilities and difficulties and will provide information with regard to the areas in which a child most needs help. Assessment, in turn, depends upon a description of precisely what kinds of ability are included under the general heading of language intervention. Planned intervention involves deliberate attempts to initiate changes in behaviour. Language intervention for mentally handicapped children will be concerned with the most effective way of producing changes in children's language, and thus requires an understanding of the mechanisms or processes which cause change. These two issues form the topics of the next chapter. Finally, throughout this text, the term 'teaching' is used to refer to any deliberate attempt to influence a child's behaviour, or encourage developmental change and, unless clearly stated, does not imply any specific theoretical or practical approach.

Information on Current Practices in Special Schools

Systematic intervention never occurs in a vacuum. Whichever special teaching procedures are advocated, it is inevitable that they will occur in association with other experiences and that they will be introduced in place of other procedures. For example, in special schools there are numerous experiences to which children are exposed during a school day which may be beneficial in terms of language acquisition. Some of these experiences may occur as part and parcel of lessons or other activities not specifically designed to promote language, for example school routines such as lunch, mid-morning drinks or playtime. Without a clear description and evaluation of the linguistic and communicative experiences a child has in school in addition to systematic language teaching activities, it may be impossible to tell whether a child learns more from structured intervention than from unstructured everyday activities which involve communication. Indeed, it may be that, in some respects, unstructured activities in which the adult's concern is with something other than language, are more helpful than structured language teaching activities (Harris, 1984a and b). Similarly before one form of structured intervention is introduced in place of an existing set of procedures for language teaching, one would need to be convinced that the new procedures were likely to be more effective. Thus, in selecting those experiences most likely to be helpful to children in acquiring language, it is important to have some idea of the existing practices within special schools and ideally, some indication of the extent to which these practices already influence language learning.

In addition to providing a setting for children's learning, special schools are characterised by an organisation and a set of procedures with enable the teachers and auxiliary staff to plan and coordinate their activities. School organisation and the activities which occur within schools both reflect the aims of special education and provide constraints within which adults continually re-interpret the meaning of special education. It is suggested that there is a close inter-dependence between the kinds of practices which occur within schools and the attitudes and beliefs which teachers have about education. Existing practices which are designed to promote language acquisition will be sustained by beliefs and attitudes about what language acquisition involves in relation to mentally handicapped children. The corollary of this is that existing practices will only be successfully replaced by new and more effective procedures for language intervention if they are also consistent with teachers' attitudes and beliefs. Needless to say any changes in organisation necessary to implement new teaching methods will also need to be compatible with the organisational system which operates in each classroom and in the school at large. New practices, no matter how potentially beneficial in terms of learning, will be unlikely to become established in schools unless they can be assimilated within the wider organisational framework of the school and are recognised as being consistent with currently held views about the aims and methods of educating mentally handicapped children (Harris, 1985).

Since the school organisation both reflects and constrains teachers' perceptions about special education, these two features of the school need to be fully understood if new methods of assessment and teaching are to be successful. If new methods challenge teachers' perceptions and their existing teaching practices, then additional intervention procedures will be necessary to reduce this incompatibility. This is likely to mean education through in-service courses to change teachers' beliefs and attitudes about children in special schools, or training staff to employ a more appropriate form of school organisation. A third possibility would involve imposing new forms of organisation and management structure from above to create an environment within which alternative perceptions and ways of working with children could flourish. However, before any of these approaches can be adopted it is necessary to have a description of the way in which special schools are organised, the practices which constitute special education and the beliefs and attitudes which sustain these practices.

In this section it has been suggested that information is needed regarding current practices in special schools. This information is necessary to determine the extent to which children in special schools are provided with environmental support for language acquisition. Such an evaluation depends upon an adequate description of day-to-day teaching practices which can be evaluated in terms of contemporary theories regarding the role of experience in language acquisition. Information on school organisation, teaching practices and teachers' perceptions of their role is also necessary to determine the extent to which innovations in practices are likely to be successful and how far it might be necessary to accompany programmes of curriculum change with strategies designed to change teacher perceptions and develop alternative methods of school organisation.

METHODOLOGICAL CONSIDERATIONS

This book describes the first part of a larger research project concerned with language learning in special schools. The first part of the project was conducted using postal questionnaires. It is concerned with a description of the physical and organisational characteristics of a large number of special schools with particular reference to language teaching. It includes a description of the ways in which teachers set out to assess children's language, different approaches to encouraging language development, and the help which is available from parents and professionals. Finally, it looks at suggestions offered by teachers for improving current practice. The second part of the project (in preparation) will use an observational approach to explore linguistic interactions in classrooms and interviews to explore teachers' perceptions of specific language learning activities for the children they work with.

Selection of Schools

The schools described in this report were initially selected from the list of Special Schools and Homes for Handicapped Pupils (Wales) in the Education Authorities Directory (1983). All schools in Wales which were identified as making provision for ESN(S) pupils, children with severe or complex learning problems, children with language and communication problems and autistic children were included. Initially 45 schools were contacted, but replies indicated that only 34 of these schools were predominantly concerned with children who could be included under the broad heading of severe mental handicap.

The Questionnaires

Head teachers in each of the schools were sent a total of four questionnaires (see Appendices). The first of these was intended to be completed by the head teacher, and was concerned with the organisation of the school as a whole, including numbers of staff and pupils, the number of classes, the availability of professional help from outside the school, contact with parents, and general questions about the language policy within the school.

The other three questionnaires were identical, although they were headed differently to assist the head teacher in distributing them to appropriate members of staff. The head was asked to distribute them to teachers who normally worked with children of 3 different levels of linguistic ability. These were: pre-verbal children; children who used predominantly single word utterances; children who used phrases and sentences. Although this may appear at first sight to be a crude strategy for identifying children with varying levels of ability, it was felt that the headings used were sufficiently straightforward, and the overall ability scale so long that it would not be difficult for respondents to be accurately located. None of the heads or class teachers indicated that they found these instructions difficult to understand or to carry out. Each of the questionnaires was accompanied by a stamped addressed envelope and it was hoped that this would encourage all the staff involved to give accurate responses even to those questions which might have been regarded as dealing with sensitive issues.

The teachers' questionnaire was concerned with the characteristics of the pupils in that teacher's class, methods of language assessment employed, strategies for language teaching, the availability of classroom help, the involvement of professional help from outside the classroom, parental participation in language work, and the teacher's qualifications and special responsibilities.

The questionnaires were extensively revised following comments and discussions with colleagues involved in special education. They were also sent to a small number of teachers in special schools to ensure that the questions were all appropriate and intelligible.

Response Rates

Of the 136 questions sent out, a total of 120 (81%) were returned. Although not all schools returned all 4 questionnaires, those included in the analysis of results all returned 3 or more questionnaires. Table 1.1 indicates the number of schools identified as making provision for severely mentally handicapped pupils (pupils with severe and complex learning difficulties) in the 8 Welsh education authorities, and the numbers of head teachers' and teachers' questionnaires returned from each. Where individual teachers failed to respond to all the items in the questionnaires, the specific responses were coded as missing, and the N in the analysis was reduced accordingly.

Table 1.1: Distribution of Target Schools and Returns for Heads' and Class Teachers' Questionnaires

Authority	No. of Schools	No. of Heads' Questionnaires Returned	No. of Teachers' Questionnaires Returned
Clwyd	6	6	15
Dyfed	4	4	11
Gwent	3	3	9
Gwynedd	5	5	13
Mid Glam.	6	6	18
Powys	1	1	3
South Glam.	5	3	9
West Glam.	4	4	10
Total	34	32	88

Chapter Two

CHILD LANGUAGE IN PERSPECTIVE: DEVELOPMENT, ASSESSMENT AND INTERVENTION

Surprisingly, there are few studies currently available which have addressed the issue of what kinds of experience are routinely provided for children in special schools. This is a broad question which needs to be asked in relation to a number of curriculum areas and developmental abilities. For practical reasons this study has focussed exclusively on those experiences which might be regarded as being relevant to the acquistion of language. This chapter presents some of the theoretical issues relating to child language and language intervention. It begins with a discussion of issues concerned with language description and the various approaches to language assessment. This is followed by an overview of different approaches to language intervention. The final section provides a brief summary of alternatives to spoken language which have been employed with mentally handicapped children.

ISSUES IN LANGUAGE ASSESSMENT

Assessment of mentally handicapped children involves providing a description of children's abilities and disabilities. However, since children are very complex there is an almost infinite range of possible descriptions which might be given for any individual child. The particular descriptions which are given will depend upon a number of assumptions including the purpose of the assessment, the criteria against which the handicapped child's performance is compared and the theoretical framework which is employed. Each of these areas will now be considered in more detail in respect of language assessments.

The Purpose of Assessment

Assessments of a mentally handicapped child's language may be carried out for a number of different reasons. First, assessments may be conducted to determine the best placement for a child either in terms of different schools or with respect to different classes within a school. Such an assessment is likely to focus on the child's ability to understand instructions and to participate in class activities which require language. A second reason for carrying out an assessment is to determine the progress a child makes over time: an initial assessment may be repeated sometime later and differences in performance compared. Such an approach may be used to provide information regarding progress or regression and the relative merit of different approaches to language teaching. In order that language measures are maximally sensitive to real changes and not influenced by teacher expectations or different degrees of familiarity with different children, it is likely that such assessments will involve procedures which require the child to respond to a pre-determined set of stimuli. A third reason for carrying out an assessment is to identify areas of language which represent the most suitable areas for teaching. Fourthly, the results of an assessment can provide the teacher with additional information which may be helpful when the child is discussed with colleagues in the school, with parents and with other professionals. Finally, assessments may be useful in that by providing the teacher with different ways of viewing the child's language they may give the teacher a better understanding of the child's difficulties. Although different types of assessments are also carried out to determine diagnosis or the aetiology of a particular disorder and also to provide information regarding prognosis, in the field of language with mentally handicapped children these are seldom realistic objectives; there are very few conditions which can be identified through an analysis of language patterns, and since the environment is so important for language development, an assessment at any point in time is unlikely to be informative about future progress.

The Criteria for Comparison

Noticing something about a child's language presupposes that the observer has a mental framework

within which it is possible to categorise and
evaluate aspects of language performance. The next
sub-section considers in more detail the ways in
which theoretically based descriptions of language
provide a detailed matrix for making choices about
levels and types of language assessment. This
section is concerned with the evaluative aspect of
language assessment and the criteria which make it
possible to identify language as appropriate or
inappropriate, advanced or delayed, normal or
deviant.

<u>Appropriate and Inappropriate Language</u>. Language
always occurs in some context and it is always
possible to make some judgement about whether it is
reasonable for an individual to produce particular
language forms within a particular setting. For
example, it is appropriate to say 'thank you' when
receiving something being offered by another person,
but it is inappropriate to say 'thank you' when
giving an object. Similarly it is appropriate to say
'goodbye' when someone is leaving and 'hello' when
meeting someone; it would be inappropriate to say
'hello' when leave-taking and 'goodbye' as a
greeting. One of the most important aspects of
language use is the ability of speakers to make
their contribution appropriate to the context and
naturally this is one of the most important aspects
of an assessment of the language of a mentally
handicapped child. Rees (1978) gives the
illustration of the child who after intensive
instruction was able to produce 'wh' questions such
as 'who is it?'; 'what is it?'; 'where is it?', and
yet was unable to modify his language to be
consistent with different contexts. As a result upon
being reminded to ask questions the child announced,
to no-one in particular, 'who is it?'; 'what is
it?'; 'where is it?' Thus even complex sentences may
not be positively evaluated within an assessment if
they are used inappropriately. On the other hand,
children with very little command of grammar and a
limited vocabulary may be able to use language
extremely successfully if they are able to modify
their language in response to the situation.

<u>Advanced and Delayed Language</u>. Clearly, the terms
'advanced' and 'delayed' imply some benchmark
against which they have some meaning. The language
of mentally handicapped children may be described as

advanced or delayed in relation to two different criteria. The first concerns implied comparisons with the language of ordinary (non-handicapped) children of a similar chronological age. Some standardised tests provide such comparisons and, in the case of a child with delayed language, a developmental quotient. Similarly, some developmental charts make it possible to describe a child's language as being similar to the language of an ordinary child of a certain chronological age. The second meaning of advanced and delayed implies some comparison with other cognitive abilities. For example a child of 10 years of age who scores on a non-verbal intelligence test at the same level as an ordinary (non-handicapped) child of 10, might have specific difficulties with language and therefore only perform on a language test as well as ordinary (non-handicapped) 4 year olds. Such a child might also be regarded as delayed in terms of language. It is also possible that a mentally handicapped child might have language which is delayed in relation both to chronological age and in relation to other areas of cognitive functioning. Alternatively, a mentally handicapped child might have language which is relatively advanced in relation to other areas of cognitive functioning. Clearly, it is necessary to be precise about the criteria which are involved when describing a child's language in terms of 'advance' and 'delay'. (See Ryan (1973) for a discussion of the difficulties involved in diagnosing such specific deficits).

Normal and Deviant Language. These terms refer to the pattern of linguistic abilities shown by a child. A child who has language which is, in all respects, like the language of a younger ordinary (non-handicapped) child may be described as displaying delayed but otherwise normal language. In contrast, a child who shows a pattern of linguistic abilities in which the different areas of language are progressing at differential rates (in comparison with the pattern of progress found among ordinary, non-handicapped children) might be described as having deviant language, that is to say this child's language does not resemble the pattern of linguistic abilities found among normal children of any age. For example Blank, Gessner and Esposito (1979) describe a child with normal development in relation to grammar and the expression of meanings but considerable impairment in respect of the functional/communicative aspects of language. (See Harris (1986) for a general discussion of delay and deviance in relation to cognitive and linguistic development).

Descriptions of Child Language and Language Assessment

In the preceding section it has been suggested that the purpose of an assessment and the criteria against which an individual child's performance is judged will determine what factors are perceived as relevant to any description of language. The third and perhaps the most important factor which contributes to 'what counts as relevant information for assessment' is the breadth of the descriptive framework for language itself. Linguists and developmental psychologists have gradually and rather painstakingly extended their conceptions of what constitutes a reasonably complete description of language to include grammatical, semantic and functional aspects (Dore, 1978; Lock, 1980). While these areas are explored in greater detail below, this section begins by drawing attention to a more widely recognised division within the field of language: the distinction between comprehension and production.

Comprehension and Production. There are two issues which deserve consideration in respect of the assessment of language production and language comprehension. The first concerns the relationship between comprehension and production during development. The conclusion that a child's ability to comprehend a sentence of a given level of complexity precedes the production of similar sentences (Fraser, Bellugi and Brown, 1973) has been shown to be at the very least premature and possibly simply wrong. Instead a more modest conclusion, and one which is more consistent with recent research studies, is that comprehension and production interact in a complex way at every stage of development and that at certain times children may produce appropriate utterances which they would have difficulty in understanding if produced by others. This serves to demonstrate a basic point; comprehension is not easier than production, rather the two are different kinds of linguistic activity involving different psychological processes (Elliot, 1981).

The second issue involves the need to consider both production and comprehension skills when assessing the linguistic abilities of mentally handicapped children. Since the two areas involve different processes it is not advisable to assume that performance in one can provide a reliable measure of performance in the other. While a child may produce relatively complex grammatical sentences, this should not be taken as evidence that the same child will understand sentences of the same level of complexity when uttered by someone else.

<u>Structural Approaches to Describing Language</u>. A language is, in part, a system for organising speech sounds into sequences which can convey meanings. Users of a language know enough rules about sound combinations to both encode novel messages into sound sequences and to decode new messages from the sound sequences they hear. Thus, an infinite number of meanings or messages can be conveyed using a finite number of speech sounds (in English there are only approximately 44 distinct speech sounds or phonemes, Hawkins, 1984). In part, the power of a language for encoding meaning derives from the hierarchical way in which sounds are organised into strings. Thus, sounds can be combined into morphemes using phonemic rules (e.g. play, clay but not vlay or xlay); morphemes can be combined into words using morphemo-grammatical rules (e.g. plurals = noun + S; adverbs = adjective plus-ly); words can be combined into sentences using syntactic rules (e.g. a simple active declarative sentence = article plus adjective plus noun plus main verb plus article plus noun). The whole system of rules for creating words and sentences from simple sounds is called a grammar and descriptions of language which are based on a grammar are called structural descriptions. Thus assessments of children's language which consider measures such as the length of the child's utterances (the mean length of utterance is a widely used index of structural complexity, Brown, 1973) the number of grammatical errors, the extent to which a child employs nouns, verbs and adjectives, and the frequency of active, declarative, interrogative and passive sentences are all based upon structural descriptions.

In this study a clear distinction is made regarding children's relative ability in producing language structures. In order to obtain data from teachers working with children with a wide range of linguistic abilities, separate questionnaires were directed at teachers in three categories; those concerned with children at the single word stage, those working with children who produce mainly two and three word phrases, and those working with children able to produce sentences. Clearly this approach is a far from perfect but it did provide a self-selection strategy for the teacher respondents which was directly related to broad kinds of productive language skills of the children they worked with.

Semantic Approaches to Describing Language. Semantic descriptions are concerned with the meanings expressed in linguistic structures. Although it is the case that language structures can convey an infinite number of meanings, it is also true that meanings which are expressed can be classified into a relatively small set. As Fillmore remarked, meanings tend to be concerned with basic aspects of events and activities in which human beings are engaged, such as 'who did it, who it happened to, and what got changed' (Fillmore, 1968, p. 24). Moreover, in the case of young children the range of semantic relations expressed in two and three word utterances seems to be even more highly restricted. For example, Brown (1973) suggested a set of 8 primary semantic relations. These included agent plus action (daddy drive, mummy eat) action plus object (drive car; kick ball) object plus location (coat chair; daddy car) agent plus object (daddy (drive) car; mummy (is making) lunch) and possessor of object possessed (my coat; daddy('s) car). More recently Braine (1976) has suggested that it may be misleading to try and describe all children's utterances in terms of a pre-defined set, since the number of potential semantic distinctions which a child could express in language is very large. Instead, Braine argues that the semantic relations which are salient for any given child should be derived from an examination of the utterances the child is currently using.

From the examples presented in parentheses above, (see particularly the three semantic relations expressed by the one structure 'daddy car'), it is clear that part of the problem of a semantic analysis lies in deciding on what meaning a child intended to convey via a structural sequence which is missing many elements considered essential in the language of adults. The accepted solution to this difficulty lies in examining the context within which an utterance occurs. It is suggested that at this stage children are restricted in their verbal communication through an imperfect knowledge of the grammatical rules necessary for producing complex sound sequences; they intend to convey more than they can put into words. If adults pay careful attention to the situation in which the child's utterances occur, and in particular, to the events which precede these utterances, then it is argued, they will be able to infer what a child actually intended to say (Bloom, 1970). In the example provided above of 'daddy car' the same structure might be interpreted as meaning 'daddy is driving the car' as daddy starts the engine and the car moves forward, 'daddy is in the car' in response to the question 'where is daddy?' and 'daddy's car' in response to the question 'what's this?' Thus a semantic description of utterances which are, from a grammatical point of view, inadequately expressed, requires not only a record of the utterances themselves but also a very careful description of the situation and events which surround each utterance. Utterances which are longer than two words may be described as strings which incorporate previously learned two-term semantic relations (Brown, 1973). For example, the sentence 'Daddy drive car work' incorporates a set of related semantic relations:

Daddy drive - agent plus action
Drive car   - action plus object
Car work   - object plus location.

At this point in development, it may also be reasonable to credit a child with knowledge of grammatical classes and syntactical rules. In this case an alternative description of the same sentence, and one which perhaps looks more familiar, would be:

Daddy   drive   car   work.
Subject   main verb   object   indirect object.

Functional Approaches to Describing Language. While structural and semantic approaches are concerned with the way in which grammatical conventions make it possible for words and sentences to carry meaning, functional approaches are specifically concerned with the relationship between language and the social context. At its most basic level this implies two additional aspects of language. First, in order to be able to use language to communicate with others a speaker must take account of the social context. This involves making numerous unconscious decisions concerning such things as when to speak, and when to be silent, how to be maximally informative without being redundant, and how to reach an agreement with another speaker/listener about what will constitute the topic of a conversation. Secondly, language use involves knowing how to use language to influence the social context. Ordinary talk implies speaking with some purpose in mind. For example, it may be the speaker's intention to persuade a listener of his point of view, to inform another of a piece of news, to reprimand or to influence that person's behaviour. Such actions can be achieved directly through the use of certain words: 'You must believe me'; 'I tell you, we're finished'; 'You were wrong to do that'; 'Please meet me at eight o'clock.' On the other hand they may be achieved indirectly. For example, it is frequently possible to deliberately influence other people's behaviour by giving them information: 'There's a fire in the basement. The fire officer said that everyone should leave the building.' The speaker of these sentences achieves a particular effect because the listeners are able to understand the implications of what has been said even though no one uttered the words 'You must leave the building now!'

The effect which a speaker intends to produce on listeners is known as the illocutionary force of an utterance and these are expressed in illocutionary acts. In the language of young children illocutionary acts tend to be relatively few in number and to be closely linked to particular grammatical forms (Halliday, 1975). However, as children get older they master a greater range of linguistic functions and they become able to express each function (or illocutionary act) using a variety of linguistic forms. Figure 2.1 shows the occurrence of different illocutionary acts in samples of speech from three year old children (Dore, 1976).

Summary

The importance of describing language in terms of structure, meaning and function has led to the introduction of a term designed to draw attention to

Table 2.1:   Illocutionary Acts Identified in the
             Speech of Three Year Olds (Dore, 1976)

Utterance Type	% of all utterances
Requests, i.e. utterances which request salient information, actions or acknowledgements	27
Responses, i.e. utterances which directly complement preceding utterances	18.5
Descriptions, i.e. utterances which represent observable or verifiable aspects of context	22.3
Statements, i.e. utterances which express analytic and institutional facts, beliefs, attitudes, emotions and reasons	13.8
Conversational Devices, i.e. utterances which regulate social interaction and conversations	5.8
Performatives, i.e. utterances which accomplish actions by being said	10.8
Uninterpretable utterances	7.9
Utterances coded for two of the above categories	5.8

these complementary levels of analysis: the speech
act (Searle, 1969; Dore, 1978). Speech acts are
actions performed through words and sentences. Such
actions are successfully completed because both
speaker and listener share background knowledge
about the conventions for expressing meaning in
words and sentences (grammatical rules) and the
conventions associated with using language within
different social contexts.

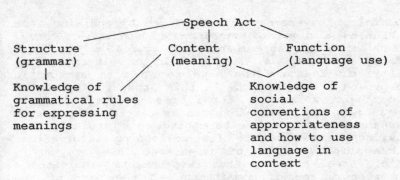

Naturally, the knowledge implied in the theory of speech acts is necessary for both speakers and listeners since it underlies both comprehension and production of language. Thus a general framework for the assessment of linguistic difficulties might include the following areas.

	Production	Comprehension
Structure/grammatical adequacy	___	___
Content/representation of meaning	___	___
Function/appropriateness and use of language in context	___	___

In the following section, different approaches to language assessment are discussed, and reference will be made to this descriptive framework. The emphasis will be upon practical aspects of assessment and different assessment instruments. The question of the validity of particular forms of assessment in the light of speech act theory are dealt with elsewhere (Harris, forthcoming).

METHODS OF LANGUAGE ASSESSMENT

Language assessment can be carried out in a wide variety of ways and for a variety of purposes. Although this section is primarily concerned with relatively formal assessments which involve teachers and speech therapists in making a permanent written record of a child's ability at a given point in time, it is obvious that a teacher may well be making informal assessments of a child's language, which are not recorded, during the ordinary day-to-day business of organising and teaching a class of mentally handicapped children. Such informal assessments may guide a teacher's daily interactions with a child or alternatively, they may indicate the need for a more systematic approach to assessment. In this study the focus has been upon relatively formal assessments which are recorded. The reason for this is partly because such assessments are easier to monitor, particularly when using a questionnaire for collecting information, than informal types of assessment. However, it is also true that written assessments indicate a greater degree of committment on the part of the teacher and, since they involve greater effort and result in a permanent record of a child's ability, their influence is likely to be greater, both within the classroom and beyond.

It is also important to recognise that, since children are changing and developing over time, assessment ought not to be considered as a discrete activity which can be completed on one occasion. Rather, assessment is a continuous process of monitoring a child's progress over time, and, where appropriate, examining this in relation to the educational experiences which are made available to the child.

In distinguishing formal assessments from informal 'on the spot' assessments, it has been suggested that the results of the former are recorded while the results of the latter are not. Additional differences include that formal assessments are conducted for a specific purpose or purposes and that formal assessments imply a specific structure or framework for looking at language. Informal assessments may be prompted simply because a teacher notices something different in a child's performance; what is noticed and the associated evaluation of its significance will be dependent upon intuitive rather than structured frameworks for interpretation. However, formal assessment procedures also differ both with respect to the degree of structure they impose on a child's linguistic ability and the way in which the structure is introduced. Assessment instruments will be considered under three general headings: standardised tests, developmental charts and profiles of linguistic ability.

Standardised Tests

Tests may be considered as standardised for two reasons: first, tests usually require that a basis for a description of a child's linguistic ability should be responses to a pre-specified set of standard stimuli. Secondly, it may be possible to compare a child's performance on the test with the performance of a large number of other children. In this case the performance of the large group, when ordered in terms of successful performance or in terms of chronological age, provides a standard measure. It is argued that comparison of one child's score with the set of standard scores enables that individual's score to be interpreted in terms of relative ability or in terms of a developmental quotient (better or worse than a given percentage of children, for example 'language at the level of an ordinary, non-handicapped child of 5 years'). Of the tests mentioned in this study, the Reynell Developmental Language Scale is a standardised test in both senses: on the comprehension scale it involves both the presentation of a standard set of stimuli and the possibility of interpreting a child's performance in terms of a simple developmental quotient scale. On the other hand, the assessment procedure incorporated within the Derbyshire Language Scheme (Knowles and Masidlover, 1982) is a standardised procedure only in so far as it involves presenting the child with a set of pre-selected stimuli.

Developmental Scales and Charts

Developmental charts do not usually require the teacher/speech therapist to present a child with particular stimulus materials. Instead they involve a person who knows the child well indicating on a list of language comprehension and production skills, those abilities which are characteristic of the child in question and those that are not. The structure is provided by the examples of language skills which are selected for inclusion within the chart, and the way in which they are ordered to represent a putative developmental sequence. Developmental scales vary both with respect to the size of the gaps between adjacent skills in the sequence and in terms of whether they are solely concerned with language or include items concerned with other areas of functioning. The developmental scales and charts referred to in this study are listed below.

Developmental Scales and Charts

Concerned only with language:	Concerned with additional areas of development as well as language:
Language charts from 'Let me Speak' Jeffree and McConkey (1976)	Sheridan 'Stycar' sequences (Sheridan, 1973)
	Gunzberg Progress Assessment Charts (1973)
Language charts produced by the Hester Adrian Research Centre, Cunningham and Jeffree (1971)	Portage checklist (Shearer and Shearer (1976)
	National Childrens Bureau Developmental Guide (1977)
Assessment scales in the Derbyshire Language Scheme (Knowles and Masidlover, 1982)	Teacher's Developmental Assessment Charts (Berry, 1978)

Language Profiles

A language profile represents an analysis of a sample of a child's spontaneous language, which provides an indication of that child's strengths and weaknesses in relation to a number of related areas of linguistic performance. Usually, the sample of speech is recorded and then transcribed prior to analysis. The profile which is used as a basis for analysis will determine both what aspects of language are included in the assessment, and the extent to which comparisons are possible across different areas of ability, and with respect to other children of a similar chronological age. The only profile mentioned in this study is the Language Assessment Remediation and Screening Profile (L.A.R.S.P.) developed by Crystal, Fletcher and Garman (1976) and Crystal (1979). It provides a detailed structure for the analysis of grammatical abilities but is very much less informative about semantic and functional areas of language.

In view of the different aims of assessment and the wide range of assessment instruments available it is important to discover what forms of assessment teachers in special schools employ and their reasons for conducting language assessments. The study also sought information regarding other people besides the teacher who were involved in assessing children and the way in which assessments were used.

LANGUAGE TEACHING

It has been suggested that language teaching involves managing the environment so that children with language difficulties are exposed to experiences which will support language acquisition. More specifically, it is suggested that the chosen method of language intervention should be demonstrably more effective than the available alternatives, even when one of the alternatives involves doing nothing or at least doing nothing which specifically focusses upon language. This section will review briefly three approaches to the teaching of language in special schools. The three approaches are the behavioural approach, the developmental training approach and the developmental processes approach. The reason for selecting these slightly unconventional terms will, it is hoped, become clear to the reader during the course of this section.

The Behavioural Approach

Advocates of the behavioural approach to teaching emphasise the distinction between 'what is taught' and 'how to teach' and generally treat the two as quite independent issues (Ruder, 1978). The answer to the question what to teach is determined by a committment to view language as verbal behaviour and to eschew more elaborate descriptions which rely upon inferences from behaviour.

It might be reasonable to infer that a child who is able to produce utterances such as 'I like dolls' 'dolls are fun to play with' 'you can do lots of things with dolls' has a fairly sophisticated knowledge of the rules of English grammar. However, a behavioural description would only be concerned with the word sequences which the child utters, their adequacy according to adult criteria and their relationship to surrounding events, for example, did the utterances occur in response to questions, was the child talking to someone (or was the child alone), and if so, what was the other person's response? The issue of adequacy is normally dealt with in terms of grammatical correctness although there is no obvious reason why other criteria might not be used instead. Thus, for those concerned with behavioural approaches, the question of what should be taught is generally answered - grammatical sentences of increasing complexity. The issue of how language relates to preceding and following events is usually considered to be bound up with the question of how best to teach language to children. Each of these two issues will now be considered in more detail.

Within a behavioural framework, the identification of complex grammatical utterances as a long-term aim for intervention has two specific limitations. First, a grammatical description, for example subject, verb, object, is not a description of specific behaviours which can be taught. Thus, in order to be amenable to teaching such an aim would need to be translated into specific sentences which could become the objectives of a teaching programme. But once this step is taken teaching is focussed upon specific strings of words and not the grammatical relations which make that string an acceptable sentence. The second limitation is that for a child with language difficulties there may be an enormous gap between present abilities and the long-term objectives. The teacher therefore needs a strategy for converting the gap between present abilities and terminal objectives into a small sequence of steps or stages so that the initial steps are likely to be attainable by the child almost immediately while the final steps culminate in the terminal objective - specific complex grammatical utterances. One strategy commonly employed within this paradigm is to break down the complex terminal objectives into learning steps which are based loosely on a grammatical analysis (Guess, Sailor and Baer, 1974; Ruder, 1978). Thus a child might initially be introduced to a group of nouns and taught to produce them in response to pictures of their referents; subsequently verbs and adjectives might be introduced in the same way, before noun verb, or noun verb adjective noun strings were taught.

Within this approach the question of how to teach language is answered with reference to the principles of operant conditioning. Essentially, it is argued that all behaviour is determined by its relationship with antecedent events (cues) and consequences (Skinner, 1957). Behaviour which is followed by events which are pleasant (e.g. encouragement, praise, physical contact, food, sweets and drinks) will tend to occur more often in the future under the same stimulus conditions (i.e. when the same cues are present). Behaviour which is followed by distressing or unpleasant events will tend to occur less often in the future under similar conditions. Through careful observation, events which have the effect of increasing the strength of behaviour may be identified, as may those events which have the effect of reducing the strength of the behaviours they follow. Once such reinforcing and punishing events have been appropriately classified, it should be possible to manipulate the relationship between specific behaviours and the events which follow them (the environmental contingencies) so that, under specific stimulus conditions, certain related behaviours are strengthened and therefore become more likely to occur in the future while others are weakened or extinguished. Language behaviours can thus be taught be reinforcing pre-selected verbal responses with an effective reinforcer - e.g. 'good boy', 'that's nice talking' or a sweet.

This approach to language teaching led to the emergence of a number of conventions regarding what constitutes good teaching practice. Among these are the following:

a)   Teaching must be based upon a clear (behavioural) specification of what is to be taught - teaching objectives must be defined in terms of observable behaviour.

b)   The teacher must seek to gain maximum control of the child's responses: only responses consistent with the teaching objectives should be encouraged.

c)   Successful teaching is dependent upon a clear structure with respect to <u>what</u> is taught and <u>how</u> appropriate responses are encouraged.

d)   A teacher will be maximally effective in teaching when he or she only has to attend to one child.

e)   A child will be more likely to attend to the relevant cues and to make the appropriate connections between his or her behaviour and the consequences, if competing stimuli are excluded. Teachers are encouraged to conduct lessons in separate rooms or in screened quiet areas within the main classroom.

Reference to these conventions is frequently made in language teaching programmes designed to be used by teachers in special schools (Harris, 1984c).

The Developmental Training Approach

This approach represents an attempt to reconcile behavioural teaching methods (how to teach) with the growing body of research evidence which suggests that ordinary children progress through a reasonably predictable sequence of stages when acquiring language, and that language acquisition involves much more than learning to produce sequences of words which conform to adult intuitions about grammatical adequacy.

In the light of this evidence, it has become apparent that an alternative way of sequencing learning steps would be to derive a curriculum from the course of language development among ordinary non-handicapped children. It is argued that, since this is the order in which ordinary children learn a series of complex skills when left to their own devices, it is also likely to be the most effective way of sequencing learning objectives for mentally handicapped children (Miller and Yoder, 1974). Furthermore, teaching a broader range of language skills in a developmental sequence is compatible with an alternative philosophical perspective - that intervention is concerned with facilitating developmental changes.

The precise developmental curricula employed has tended to reflect contemporary research on language acquisition among ordinary children. Following Chomsky's work on transformational grammar, programmes were devised to teach phrase structure and transformational rules. Later research on the grammatical rules reflected in children's language indicated that some early two-word combinations might be represented by very simple rules of the type:

$$\text{Sentence} = \begin{array}{l} P_1 + 0 \\ 0 + P_2 \\ 0 + 0 \end{array}$$

$$\begin{array}{ll} \text{Where } P &= \text{pivot} \\ 0 &= \text{open} \end{array}$$

$$\begin{array}{ll} P_1 &= \text{more, no, there} \\ P_2 &= \text{gone, eat, give} \\ 0 &= \text{mummy, daddy, ball, cake (Braine, 1963)} \end{array}$$

Subsequently, these rules provided the content of teaching programmes designed for mentally handicapped children.

When it became clear that early word combinations could be more usefully described in terms of semantic relations such as Agent and Action, Action and Object, these too were incorporated into teaching programmes. Finally, the emergence of functional descriptions presented programme designers with a new set of curriculum objectives (Rees, 1978). While the developmental training approach increasingly drew upon the developmental literature to guide the selection and sequencing of objectives within training programmes, this was accomplished alongside a continuing adherence to behavioural teaching strategies. Hence, by implication these approaches advocated the contradictory thesis of teaching language development through the modification of target behaviours (see Harris, 1984a). It should be noted that the interpretation of 'teaching' within a behavioural paradigm is very different from that presented in the rest of this book, where teaching is deliberately more loosely defined as the selection and management of learning opportunities.

The Developmental Processes Approach
More recently, research on the social interactional processes which seem both to precede and to create the conditions for language development (Bruner, 1983) indicated ways in which intervention might be directed at supporting such processes rather than attempting to circumvent them through direct instruction.

Contemporary research suggests three areas which are particularly important regarding the processes implicated in early language acquisition. Each of these areas will be considered briefly.

Social and Cognitive Prerequisites. Viewed as a developmental phenomena it is clear that spoken language does not arrive from nowhere, but is preceded by a period of non-verbal preparation. From birth up to the age of about 18 months children are seen as being engaged in frequent and often intense periods of interaction with the physical and social world. Babies are objects of considerable interest to adults and children; they are spoken to, touched, caressed and cuddled; they need to be fed, bathed,

31

changed, dressed and undressed. During all these activities babies are generally treated as individual personalities who are capable of understanding (Stern, 1977). As babies gain voluntary control of their limbs they increasingly manipulate and explore those parts of the physical environment with which they they come into contact. These experiences are seen as providing the infant with important opportunities for understanding relationships in the physical world (Piaget, 1970) and the nature of social interaction and communication (Schaffer, 1971; Newson and Newson, 1973; Bruner, 1983).

In the first 18 months of life, through repeated manipulation and exploration of the physical world and participation in social activities, children attain an understanding of physical space, the physical boundaries of their own bodies, and the implications of moving their bodies through space (for example, to move towards one object, inevitably involves moving away from other objects). Children begin to show an understanding of the way in which objects can be positioned in respect of each other (on top, underneath, inside, etc.) and the fact that similar actions on objects can be performed by different individuals. They begin to understand the properties of inanimate objects (e.g. relatively permanent, dependent upon animate beings for movement) and to distinguish these from animate objects such as people or animals (which move of their own volition, make noises and respond to sounds and actions). They also develop an understanding of their own capabilities as causal agents - that is as individuals who have the capacity to act intentionally in order to achieve specific outcomes. Such outcomes may be physical in nature, for example, grasping a book or throwing a ball, or they may be social, for example, indicating a need or request, possibly by pointing to a desired object, showing or giving an object to another person (Bates, 1976). These last mentioned social behaviours are indicative of sophisticated forms of pre-verbal communication which, it has been suggested, incorporate much of the knowledge and many of the skills underlying linguistic communication (Bruner, 1975; Bates, 1976).

An additional important communicative ability concerns reciprocity - that is making a response contingent upon the nature of the preceding contribution by the other person. Reciprocity is an essential characteristic of language in so far as most spoken language occurs in conversation with others. Conversations involve not only talking, but listening to another person and making one's own contribution 'fit in' with what has just been said. This is a complex skill which is not fully mastered until well after the advent of spoken languge (McTear, 1985; Ochs and Schieffelin, 1979, 1983). However, at the pre-verbal stage, reciprocity is clearly evident in terms of the child's emerging ability to attend to adults' language or actions and to respond during appropriate pauses. This is referred to as turn-taking and is just as crucial for successful non-verbal interactions between infants and adults as it is for spoken conversations between adults (Stern, 1977; Schaffer, 1977).

Simplified Linguistic Input. The language spoken by adults tends to be very complex for two reasons. First, it is governed by a highly abstract set of grammatical rules and, secondly, when adults converse with each other, their language rarely provides a clear or accurate representation of those rules. Instead, their language is distorted by hesitations, false starts, incomplete sentences and inappropriate coordinations of phrases. Provided with such a model, it is difficult to see how children could ever figure out the relationship between the spoken forms (the surface structure) and the meanings which they express (the deep structure). However, research has indicated that when adults address children they introduce systematic modifications into their language. These modifications include such features as higher pitch, exaggerated intonation, greater repetition, a restricted vocabulary, shorter utterances, fewer grammatical errors, simpler sentences and reference to the objects and events which are in the immediate environment (Broen, 1972; Bohannon and Marquis, 1977; Snow and Ferguson, 1977; De Paulo, Bellam and Bonvillian, 1978). It has been suggested that such simplifications make it easier for children to establish the underlying relationships which link utterances to meanings.

Specifically children may identify the meanings of individual words in sentences (that is the objects and events in their surroundings to which the words refer) and then use their knowledge of the physical and social world to work out what the speaker is trying to communicate - that is, the meaning of the sentence. Once they have determined

the likely meaning of the sentence from contextual
cues, they work backwards to figure out how specific
grammatical devices (word order; prepositions; noun
verb agreements) express such meanings (MacNamara,
1972). Note that such an explanation requires both
that children have already learned the referential
meanings associated with a range of words and
secondly, that their non-verbal knowledge of the
world is organised in such a way that it maps onto
the meanings expressed in sentences. This last point
continues to be contentious and various authors have
indicated that there is a considerable gap between a
practical understanding of events, for example, that
different people can perform the same action, and
knowledge of the associated abstract linguistic
concepts, for example, the notion of 'agents'
(Bowerman, 1976).

Offsetting these objections to some extent is
the evidence from experimental and naturalistic
studies that variations in the language of adults is
associated with different types of language among
children (Nelson, 1973) and with differential rates
or progress (Cross, 1977, 1978; Wells, 1979).
Intervention studies in which adults have been
trained to produce certain kinds of simplified
utterances have also been found to influence the
language development of both normal (Nelson, 1977)
and mentally handicapped children (Chesaldine and
McConkey, 1979). Thus, although simplified adult
language does not provide a complete explanation of
how children bridge the gap between a practical
understanding of objects and events and how such
relations can be expressed through linguistic
concepts, it does seem to be a key ingredient which
contributes to developmental progress.

The Social Context of Communicative Interactions.
Some reference has already been made to the
essentially social nature of communication in
general and linguistic communication in particular.
A central feature of any communicative exchange is
the expectation of influencing another individual;
thus communication presupposes an understanding of
what certain actions or sounds can mean for other
people and a decision to perform those actions or
sounds in order to evoke those meanings (see Searle,
1969 and Shotter, 1975 for a more detailed
discussion of communicative interactions).

The question then arises as to how infants and
young children can become aware of themselves as

beings capable of having social interactions. One solution to this problem is that babies develop intentionality as a result of observing other people respond to their unintentional or haphazard actions <u>as if they were intentional</u> (Ryan, 1974; Shotter, 1975; Newson, 1979). In the same way, at a later stage, particular actions (e.g. reaching for an object) may be attributed special social significance and thus take on the characteristics of gestures (in this case pointing) (see Lock, 1978 for a further discussion of how actions become gestures).

When children begin to use spoken language the responses of their conversational partners determine the possibilities for meaning. The range of referential meanings associated with particular words in child speech frequently bears only a rough correspondence to the meanings in adult language (Clark, 1983) and adult responses and re-interpretations are an important source of evidence for confirming or rejecting initial hypotheses about such word-referent associations. When children begin to use multi-word utterances to express semantic relations (for example Agent and Action) adult responses may provide the child not only with evidence of how successful he or she was in expressing specific meanings, but a clear indication of what in fact can be meant by such constructions. Similarly, in respect of the pragmatic aspects of language, it is the ability and willingness of adults to participate in communication games with children and respond appropriately to early utterances that demonstrates the potential which language has for influencing people (Bruner, 1983). In each situation the communicative possibilities inherent in language are realised through the social responsiveness of the child's conversational partner. The behaviour of the conversational partner is determined by what the child says, and more importantly, by the way in which the social and physical setting can be used to provide a plausible interpretation of what the child might have meant. At this point it is important to reiterate that in fact the child may not be clear about any precise intended meaning - the child's contribution is more in keeping with an exploration regarding what can be communicated linguistically and how meanings are related to utterances. The meanings expressed are constrained by the adult's interpretation in two ways. First, since there can be no communication and hence no intention to communicate outside a social setting (Meade, 1934) the possibilities for communicating meanings are a reflection of previous social encounters. Secondly, any specific intention realised in action or language may be successful or unsuccessful - it may be confirmed or refuted as an effective procedure by the adult's response (Ryan, 1974).

Since the child's utterance alone is inadequate to express meaning, the adult's interpretation will be determined by those features of the setting which are regarded as being relevant. Thus, the interpretation will depend upon the actual physical and social setting and the adult's perception of the setting in relation to figuring out what the child is trying to communicate. It follows, therefore, that different settings and different activities will create different possibilities for both the expression of meanings by the child and the comprehension of meanings by the adult. Furthermore, the adult's reason for engaging the child in social interaction and the adult's interpretation of the purpose of the activity will also influence the meanings attached to actions and utterances.

A number of studies have shown how the language of both adults and children is related to specific activities, (Wood, McMahon and Cranstoun, 1980, Tizard and Hughes, 1984) and Bruner (1983) has discussed the way in which certain activities foster communication. For example, when an adult and a young child (aged about 18 months) read a book together, the routine of sitting together and turning the pages helps to establish exactly what is being talked about. Furthermore, the structure of the activity and its repetitive nature makes it easier for the adult to predict the child's linguistic response. Together these characteristics increase the chances of the adult being able to determine what the child is attempting to say, even if articulation is poorly developed. On the other hand, conventional expectations about what meanings are appropriate to the activity of book reading means that whatever the child says will be subjected to a relatively narrow range of possible interpretations and should the child be attempting to say something unrelated to that activity, the chances of his intentions being recognised are reduced (see Scollon, 1979).

Language acquisition has been described here as a developmental phenomenon which is based upon earlier social and cognitive achievements. It also depends upon the child engaging in social interactions with others who employ simplified language forms when addressing the child. This developmental view of the processes which mediate language acquisition in children has important implications for language intervention. It suggests that it may be inappropriate to try and accommodate language to an instructional model in which learning outcomes must be specified in advance. Instead, it indicates that the focus of intervention should be the kinds of social interaction which will facilitate both pre-verbal and linguistic communication. Mentally handicapped children should be encouraged to participate in social activities which will promote the development of communicative procedures such as turn-taking, and the establishment of the adult's and the child's attention on a common topic. It is suggested that it is only through relatively unstructured social activities that the child will be able to find ways of expressing communicative intent. Similarly, it is only within a context which is established via social interaction, that an adult will be able to infer plausible interpretations of the child's meaning and reflect back to the child the linguistic structures which best capture that meaning. In short, naturalistic social routines provide the best setting for the operation of what Bruner (1983) has termed the Language Acquisition Support System (LASS). While this system seems to be effective in assisting language learning among non-handicapped children, it remains to be seen how far such a system may need to be 'tuned up' in order to be maximally effective for children with language difficulties.

Developmental Processes and the Social Context of Schools. It is often suggested that children's first utterances can be interpreted in the light of contextual cues - that is in terms of the physical setting and the social activities which occur within that setting. However, the foregoing discussion suggests that context is only important in so far as it is interpreted by the participants within any communicative exchange. In this sense context is a psychological construct rather than a characteristic of the world 'out there'. In so far as context is socially constructed (Ochs and Schieffelin, 1979; Walkerdine, 1982). It extends beyond the physical boundaries of any particular setting. Instead any activity may be described as occurring, within a nested set of contexts each of which interacts with the others (Hinde, 1986; Markova, 1986). Thus, in the special school, the classroom, the school and the wider community represent different levels of context. It is suggested that a single psychological context arises from the way in which individuals use their knowledge of different physical and social settings to arrive at interpretations of meaning. In the special school an adult may use a specific activity within a classroom setting to interpret the meanings of actions and utterances performed by a child. These communicative exchanges occur within the larger setting of the school and it is the idea of formal education and teaching which determines such things as the organisation of the classroom, the materials available and the particular activities which are sanctioned as being educational. The setting for the school is the wider community which sustains general ideas about the value of education, the need to identify and assess mentally handicapped children and to provide them with education in special schools. Alongside the public in the wider community are the professional and administrative organisations which provide a more detailed specification of the role of schools and teachers in relation to mentally handicapped children (Tomlinson, 1981).

This extended discussion of the social context of communicative interactions has been included for three reasons. First, it emphasises that language occurs as part of a social process; consequently, those concerned with language intervention must come to terms with language as a reflection of the social and psychological contexts within which it occurs. Adopting formal didactic teaching methods to encourage natural language is contradictory, since the language that will occur in such settings will be a reflection of whatever procedures are considered appropriate to formal teaching. The greater the emphasis on structured teaching the less natural is the language likely to be (see Harris, 1984a). Secondly, it underlines the importance of studying language of children in special schools within the naturally occurring settings. Thirdly, it emphasises the role of teacher in the social construction of meaning and the necessity of addressing directly both what teachers do to promote the language of mentally handicapped children and their reasons for doing it.

Table 2.2: Social and Psychological Contexts for Language and Communication in Special Schools

Context 'levels'	Instrumental effects
The community (including the public and professionals)	Recognition of mental handicap. Social stigma from labelling and separate schooling. The value of formal education and the need for special schools. Notions of delay and deviance.
Special Schools	The practice of education - formal instruction; language as a subject for teaching. Assessment of abilities.
The Classroom	Teaching activities - reflect the 'meaning' of language and language development. Importance of record keeping to gauge progress.
Specific activities	Teacher expectations of the child in terms of language and behaviour - defines the lesson context. Teachers' interpretation of the child's actions and utterances enable meanings to be assigned: interpretations enable teachers to reflect back meanings to the child.

THE LANGUAGE CURRICULUM IN SPECIAL SCHOOLS: DESIGN
AND IMPLEMENTATION

Numerous curriculum packages designed to promote
communication and language among mentally
handicapped children have been published during the
past twenty or thirty years. Many of those have been
reviewed recently and readers wishing for
descriptions of the most widely used approaches are
referred to Kiernan (1984) and Harris (1984c). This
section will consider the common features and some
of the differences between curriculum packages
before presenting a discussion of the advantages and
disadvantages of their use in special schools.

Curriculum packages for language and
communication are designed to give teachers or
parents guidance regarding activities which will
promote specific abilities among children with a
range of language difficulties. For this reason they
are also often referred to as language programmes
although there is considerable variation with
respect to the level of detail provided in the
teaching instructions. The activities suggested are
usually derived from a particular theoretical
position which in turn influences both the content
of the materials to be presented and the way in
which it is suggested that adults work with
children. The content of language teaching
programmes has mirrored the theoretical advances in
respect of how best to describe children's language
(see above). Some of the older programmes focus
exclusively on teaching grammar (language
structures) while the more recent programmes include
semantic relations and to some extent pragmatic
functions. The method of encouraging language also
varies from those that rely exclusively upon
behavioural methods in one-to-one teaching settings
to those that are more concerned with facilitating
communicative processes within relatively
naturalistic settings. Furthermore, some more
general curriculum packages, for example the Portage
scheme, indicate language skills as one sub-section
within a much wider ranging curriculum.

In general teaching packages assume little
understanding of theoretical issues by the user and
make only modest attempts to explain the ideas on
which they are based. Very little consideration is
given to the teacher's perceptions of the programme
and the extent to which the suggested ways of
working are consistent with either teachers'

understanding of language and language development
or the existing organisation of the school. There
are a number of reasons for this. First, it seems
that in the past teachers have been regarded as
simply the means by which a curriculum is delivered
to the pupils. Little attention seems to have been
given to the active part played by teachers in
choosing a programme, integrating the programme
guidelines with respect to existing classroom
practices and modifying the programme in the light
of the perceived needs of individual children.
Secondly, the majority of programmes seem to have
been conceived and developed outside the classroom
and only introduced to teachers and pupils for field
trials when it is too late to introduce major
revision (Harris, 1986).

Among the most serious limitations of most
programmes designed to promote language and
communication is that they have not been properly
evaluated in terms of their success in promoting
specific abilities among mentally handicapped
children (Kiernan, 1984; Harris, 1984c).
Furthermore, from a theoretical position there is
good reason to be cautious about the effectiveness
of the more highly structured instructional
programmes (Harris, 1984a).

In the light of these criticisms it is
important to discover to what extent language
programmes are employed in schools and how they are
used by class teachers. Where teachers do not employ
published language packages it is important to
discover what experiences they provide for children,
why they choose to tackle language and communication
in this way, and to what extent different approaches
are consistent with contemporary views about
language development. The study was also designed to
gather information regarding how teachers themselves
feel they can best be helped to be more effective in
encouraging language and communication.

ALTERNATIVES TO SPOKEN LANGUAGE

Although the majority of ordinary non-handicapped
children develop spoken language, it has been
suggested that for children who have difficulty with
oral communication, including many mentally
handicapped children, sign language or symbol
systems can offer important alternative methods of
communicating. Alternative approaches to spoken
language may be considered in terms of the extent to

which they employ abstract forms for representing experience (Kiernan, 1982). For example, symbols comprising pictorial representations of real objects are regarded as being relatively low in terms of abstraction while many of the signs employed in American Sign Language (Amslan) or British Sign Language (BSL) are regarded as being highly abstract since they have only arbitrary associations with the concepts they represent.

Sign languages make use of a distinctive set of signs which do not have a one-to-one correspondence with words in English and a system for combining signs which is not directly interpretable into English grammar. Signs are generally made with hands, arms and fingers and can be characterised in terms of four parameters: movement, hand shape, hand location and hand oriention (Kyle and Woll, 1982). On these criteria, sign languages have the status of distinct language systems (Kiernan, 1982; Musselwhite and St. Louis, 1982).

In contrast, symbol systems employ pictures and diagrams external to the body which are located in some form of frame or on a screen. The symbols themselves may be strongly iconic - that is they may physically resemble the objects or events they represent - or they may be abstract diagrams. Traditional orthography (written language) may be regarded as a relatively sophisticated symbol system which lies at one extreme on the continuum which runs from iconic to abstract representation. As with sign languages, it is possible to combine symbols into ordered sequences to convey more elaborate 'sentence' meanings. While sign languages such as Amslan and BSL tend to employ abstract signs, they also have some signs which are strongly iconic. Similarly, although symbol systems tend to employ pictures and stylised images of real objects, they inevitably need to employ more abstract diagrams for concepts which cannot be easily demonstrated with a picture.

In a survey of the approaches to non-verbal communication employed in special schools in the United Kingdom, Jones, Reid and Kiernan (1982) found that 80% of schools reported some use of signs and symbols. Of the schools which used signs, over 90% employed the Makaton vocabulary (Walker and Armfield, 1982) while about 5% employed the Paget Gorman Sign System. Approximately 30% of the schools used a symbol system; the most frequently reported systems were Bliss Symbolics (74%) and the Rebus system (26%). Each of these systems will be briefly described.

Makaton Vocabulary. Makaton is essentially a much simplified form of BSL which was first developed to help deaf mentally handicapped adults. It focusses upon 350 BSL signs in a putative developmental sequence and its aim is to provide students with a core vocabulary of useful concepts/words which can be used to meet a range of communicative needs (Walker and Armfield, 1982). It is not, therefore, a 'language' in the sense that Amslan and BSL are languages.

The Paget Gorman Sign System. In contrast to Makaton, Gorman Sign System (PGSS) employs specially designed signs which are different from those employed in BSL. However, it is claimed that PGSS provides a system for combining signs into sentence-like sequences which mirror word order in spoken English. Furthermore, PGSS is able to express all the grammatical inflexions of spoken English. For these reasons it is suggested as being particularly suitable for teaching communication in conjunction with spoken English, especially in cases where students are expected to progress to oral language (Rowe, 1982).

Bliss Symbolics. Bliss symbolics was invented by an Austrian chemist, Charles Bliss who wished to develop a universal language. It was subsequently developed for use by handicapped people by Shirley McNaughton of the Ontario Crippled Children's Centre in the 1960's. It employs both idealised pictorial representation (e.g. ⊢ = chair) and more abstract symbols (the symbol for action ∧ is based on volcancoes 'one of the primeval actions of our earth' Bailey and Jenkinson quoting Bliss, 1982). Symbols are usually presented on some form of communication board or screen and the student communicates by pointing to either single symbols or to a number of symbols in succession.

Rebus Symbols. Rebus symbols are pictorial repesentations which suggest the name of a word, for example, a picture of a bee is the rebus symbol for the verb 'be' (Kiernan, 1982). However, where Rebus

43

systems have been employed with mentally handicapped people, this relation between a picture and two homonyms has been regarded as too complex, and there is greater emphasis on simple pictorial representations of real objects (Van Oosterom, 1982).

Each of the signs and symbol systems has advantages and disadvantages for use with mentally handicapped children. Considerable claims have been made for Makaton regarding its effectiveness in establishing communicative skills in previously non-communicating children (Walker and Armfield, 1982) although these have been disputed (Kiernan, 1984). The extensive use of Makaton in special schools seems to be attributable to organisation and marketing (Walker and Armfield, 1982; Kiernan, 1984). The Makaton vocabulary is presented enthusiastically in a one day training workshop and it is claimed that teachers can learn enough in one day to begin using Makaton in the classroom. The workshops are also supported in schools and clinics by a network of regional representatives.

Because the syntax of PGSS mirrors the syntax of English, it is claimed that it is not so much an alternative to spoken English, as a complementary system which may facilitate the emergence of spoken language or extend the range of oral language skills for those children who have already begun to speak. Similarly, Bliss symbolics may be used as an alternative to spoken language, especially for those who have the potential to learn large vocabularies (Musselwhite and St. Louis, 1982) or to augment and extend existing abilities (Bailey and Jenkinson, 1982). Bliss, and to a lesser extent Rebus Systems, may be particularly suitable for some mentally handicapped children because they allow the expression of complex messages without the need for fine motor control of either the mouth and larynx or the hands (Musselwhite and St. Louis, 1982). For others the advantage of symbols over signs may result from the provision of static visual symbols which rely upon recognition of meaning - symbol relationships rather than recall, as is the case

SUMMARY

This chapter has provided an overview of recent research concerning language assessment and language intervention in special schools. The first part of the chapter considered various aspects of language assessment including why assessments are carried out, the criteria for evaluation and the kinds of linguistic information which might be included in an assessment. Three types of assessment instrument were described, standardised tests, developmental charts and language profiles.

The second part of the chapter described different approaches to language intervention: the behavioural approach, the developmental training approach and the developmental processes approach. Following a brief critique of previous attempts to initiate curriculum change in special schools the chapter concluded with a summary of different non-vocal methods of communication for mentally handicapped children. Having reviewed the main theoretical issues pertaining to language assessment and language intervention it is now possible to turn to more practical questions. Before considering in detail the ways in which teachers assess language and organise opportunities for language learning, it is necessary to describe the physical, organisational and staffing conditions which exist in special schools since these provide the immediate context for all educational activities.

Chapter Three

THE SCHOOL AS A SETTING FOR LANGUAGE DEVELOPMENT

The transfer of responsibility for children with severe learning difficulties from the Department of Health to the D.E.S. brought with it a statutory obligation for the local education authorities to make educational provision for all mentally handicapped children. From this point on, the developmental needs of such children, including their needs in respect of opportunities for language learning, were to be met within the school. In the preceding chapter it was suggested that language acquisition is an outcome of social processes and that for this reason it is particularly sensitive to the social and physical context. Schools provide a context for language development which is already shaped by the design of the buildings, the way in which children are organised into teaching groups and the expectations of teachers regarding the forms of educational experiences which will be most beneficial. This chapter begins to describe the context of language learning within special schools by focussing on the pupils and the school staff. This is followed by a discussion of the teacher's formal responsibilities in respect of language and communication, the use of sign and symbol systems in the schools and the way in which language activities are integrated within the school day.

THE PUPILS

This first section provides an overview of the numbers and general characteristics of the pupils within the schools. It emphasises the enormous variability among children in these schools and the difficulties posed by any attempt to group them into classes or groups on the basis of age, ability or educational need.

The 32 schools included in the study varied in size with the largest two schools catering for 186 and 123 pupils respectively, while the smallest was in fact a special class of 7 pupils attached to an ordinary Roman Catholic Infant/Junior Primary School. The mean number of pupils per school was 54, although this has little significance when viewed against the considerable range in the numbers of pupils attending individual schools.

The size of a class clearly imposes constraints in terms of what kinds of activity can be introduced and the possibility of working with small groups or with individual children. The returns for the teachers sampled in each school indicated that the numbers of pupils per class varied from as low as two to as high as fourteen. There are no statistically significant differences in class size across the three language levels identified in the questionnaires (see Table 3.1).

Table 3.1: The Number of Pupils Per Class

No. of Pupils per Class	No. of Pre-verbal Classes	No. of Single Words Classes	No. of Sentences Classes	Total Classes
2	0	0	1	1
4	1	1	1	3
5	1	3	1	5
6	5	2	3	10
7	4	4	2	10
8	4	8	4	16
9	7	4	3	14
10	4	5	6	15
11	1	1	5	7
12	2	1		3
14	1		3	4
Mean	8.76	5.9	9.0	8.4

One-way Analysis of Variance, Pupils per class x class type, $df = 2$, $F = 1.113$, $p \leqslant 0.327$ NS.

The extent to which the larger numbers in some classes was ameliorated by the availability of extra staff is discussed later in this chapter.

Pupils' Special Needs

Asking the teaching staff to provide details of individual pupils from medical and psychological reports was considered to be impractical and of doubtful relevance to the goal of exploring staff perceptions of their role in relation to the pupils. The simple alternative was to ask 'what categories of handicap are included among the children in the school/your class'. A set of descriptions was provided in the questionnaire which enabled the head teachers and the class teachers to estimate the numbers of children involved (see Tables 3.2 and 3.3).

Twenty-three of the thirty-two head teachers thought that the majority of their pupils were either severely mentally handicapped or were suffering from mental handicap plus an additional visual, auditory or physical handicap. More interestingly, over ten Heads indicated that in their view at least 1 of their pupils was experiencing only physical handicap, only sensory handicap or only behaviour problems.

Table 3.2: Heads' Perception of the Special Needs of
           their Pupils

Type of Special Need	Majority of Pupils	Some of Pupils	One or Two Pupils	None
Mental Handicap only	9	16	0	7
Physical Handicap only		11	1	20
Sensory Handicap only		6	4	22
Behaviour Problems only		6	4	22
Mental Handicap Plus One Other	14	17	1	0

A similar pattern emerged from the returns provided by the teachers with respect to the children in their classes. Overall, six children were identified as having only a sensory handicap and one child was identified as having only behaviour problems. None of the schools concerned was designated as making special provision to help children with these particular needs. Clearly these data may be criticised on methodological grounds since it is notoriously difficult to collect reliable information on individual children using a questionnaire. On the other hand, since one third of the Heads and about 10% of the teachers indicated that there were children in their schools who, on the basis of the 1971 and 1981 Education Acts, were inappropriately placed, it is suggested that this finding warrants further more detailed research.

Table 3.3: Categorisation of Pupils With Different Types of Handicap by Class Teachers

	Pre-verbal		Single Words		Sentences		Total	
	N	%	N	%	N	%	N	%
Mental Handicap Only	52	20.7	88	36.5	105	41.3	245	32.6
Physical Handicap Only	2	0.7	3	1.2	1	0.3	6	0.7
Sensory Handicap Only	1	0.4	2	0.8	0	0	3	0.3
Behaviour Problem Only	0	0	0	0	1	0.3	1	0.1
Mental Handicap Plus at Least One Other	196	78	148	61.4	147	57.9	496	66
TOTALS	251		241		254		751	

One-way ANOVA Pupils Handicap by level of language:
Mencap, $df = 2$, $F = 2.776$, $p \leqslant 0.068$ NS
Mencap plus, $df = 2$, $F = 1.416$, $p \leqslant 0.248$ NS

The data from the class teachers (Table 3.3) also indicates a tendency for the type of handicap

49

to be distributed according to language level. The highest proportion of mentally handicapped 'only' children occurs in the 'sentences' classes, with progressively lower percentages in the 'single' words and the 'pre-verbal' classes. Conversely, the percentage of children identified as mentally handicapped with at least one other handicap is highest in the 'pre-verbal' classes slightly lower in the 'single words' classes and lowest in the 'sentences' classes. Neither of these distributions across the different types of class reached statistical significance (p ⩽.05) when subjected to a one-way analysis of variance.

The Ages of the Pupils

The 1,727 pupils in the schools ranged in age from 2 years to 21 years. Across schools, the age of the youngest child varied from 2 years to 11 years with a mean of 3 years and 9 months. The age of the oldest pupil in the schools varied from 5 years to 21 years with a mean of 17.8 years. However, by no means all of the schools had pupils at the extreme ends of the age range; nine schools had no children over the age of 16 years. In contrast, in one school there were thirty pupils of 5 years of age or less and another school had thirty-one pupils over the age of 16 years. The mean number of pre-school age pupils for the thirty-two schools was just over four, while the mean for pupils over the age of 16 years was 8.5.

There was a similarly wide age range within the individual classes. Both the oldest child (aged 21 years) and the youngest child (aged 2 years) were reported by teachers of pre-verbal classes (Tables 3.4 and 3.5) and in fact there was a statistically significant trend for the age range of pupils within classes to decrease systematically across the three levels of linguistic ability. (One way analysis of variance df = 2, F = 9.149, p ⩽.003). This trend presumably reflects the fact that whereas the entry requirement for admission to the pre-verbal classes is primarily based upon chronological age, progress to the 'single words' and 'sentences' classes is based upon developmental progress. This selection procedure, coupled with very high individual variation in terms of speed of development would inevitably lead to the kind of distribution shown in Tables 3.4 and 3.5. It might be expected that these pupils identified by the teachers of the 'pre-verbal' children as multiply handicapped (that is suffering from mental handicap and at least one other handicapping condition) would be those who would remain longest in those classes. This distribution of pupils within the schools in relation to chronological age and severity of handicap is likely to have considerable implications for classroom management in general and the organisation of specific teaching activities (see Chapter Five below).

Table 3.4: The Chronological Ages of the Oldest Pupils in Each Class Category (in months)

	Pre-verbal	Single Words	Sentences	Total
Mean	157.7	150.96	163.3	157.4
Range	199	183	175	200

One-way ANOVA CA by Language level of class, df = 2, F = 0.391, p $\leqslant$ 0.677

Table 3.5: The Chronological Ages of the Youngest Pupils in Each Class Category (in months)

	Pre-verbal	Single Words	Sentences	Total
Mean	80.4	96.65	119.8	98.46
Range	168	173	186	191.0

One-way ANOVA CA by Language level of class, df = 2, F = 4.857, p $\leqslant$ 0.01

THE TEACHING STAFF

Overall there were 215 teachers in the schools (exclusive of non-teaching heads). This represents one teacher for every eight children, although this ratio varied across schools from one teacher to eleven pupils to one teacher for every four pupils. Individual schools employed between one and sixteen teachers and of the 88 teachers who completed the questionnaire (Table 3.6), the smallest class was just two pupils and the largest 14 (mean 8.4).

Table 3.6: Number and Sex of Teachers in Three Class Categories

	Pre-verbal	Single Words	Sentences	Total
Male	6	4	5	15
Female	23	24	24	71
Total	29*	28*	29	86

* Missing data on this variable = 2,
Total No. Teachers = 88

Teachers' Qualifications

One of the most obvious effects of the 1971 Act was to emphasise the importance of special schools being staffed by qualified teachers. The shift towards a professionally qualified teaching staff has taken place gradually, partly through in-service courses, designed to provide existing staff with opportunities to obtain relevant qualifications, and partly through a policy of only appointing new members of staff who have already completed their professional training.

On the basis of the information supplied by the head teachers, 79% of the teaching staff had initial teaching qualifications, although this ranged from as low as 25% in some schools to as high as 100% in others (see Table 3.7). The sample of 88 teachers who returned questionnaires mirrored this general pattern of initial training qualifications. Most had been awarded a Certificate in Education or a Bachelors Degree in Education. Three teachers held a Postgraduate Certificate in Education, and ten had no initial training qualification (see Table 3.8).

Table 3.7: Teachers' Qualifications and Experience (All teaching staff based on head teachers' questionnaire)

Qualifications/ Experience	N	Range within Schools	Mean within Schools	%
Initial teaching (Cert.Ed., B.Ed., P.G.C.E.)	170	1 -16	5.3	79
Special Education	45	0(8)* - 9	1.84	21
Mental Handicap	57	0(10)*-11	1.84	26.5
Others	3	0(29)*- 1	.09	1.4
Attendance on Courses for Language and Communication	14	0(18)*- 9	1.6	6.5
Teachers able to use Signs/Symbol System in Class	128	0(2)* -12	4.13	59.5

* Figures in brackets indicate numbers of schools with no teachers in each category.

Table 3.8: Initial Teaching Qualifications (based on class teachers' questionnaires)

	Pre-verbal	Single Words	Sentences	Total
Instructors	0	0	1	1
Certificate in Education	24	21	19	64
Bachelor of Education	2	4	4	10
Post-graduate Certificate in Education	1	2	0	3
No Initial Teaching Qualification	3	2	5	10
Total	30	29	29	88

Just over 55% of these teachers held an additional qualification relevant to the care and education of mentally handicapped children (Table 3.9), while only 18% had been on courses concerned with spoken language and communication in the preceding year (Table 3.10). In contrast 62% of the teachers had been on courses concerned with signing and symbol systems at some time, and the majority of these (over 80%) had attended courses on the Makaton Vocabulary (see Table 3.11).

Table 3.9: Teachers with Qualifications in Special Education or Mental Handicap

Qualifications	Pre-verbal			Single Words			Sentences			Total		
	FT	PT	TOT	FT	PT	TOT	FT	PT	TOT	FT	PT	TOT
Special Education	6	1	7	6	1	7	2	2	4	14	4	18
Mental Handicap	6	1	7	9	1	10	11	1	12	26	3	29
Other Forms of Handicap	-	-	-	1	-	1	1	-	1	2	-	2

FT = full time course: PT = part time course.

Table 3.10: Teachers who had Attended Courses on Language and Communication During Preceding Year

Courses	Pre-verbal	Single Words	Sentences	Total
With Qualification	1	-	-	1
With no Qualification	6	4	5	15
No Courses	23	25	24	72

Table 3.11: Teachers who had Attended Courses on Signing and Symbol Systems

Courses	Pre-verbal	Single Words	Sentences	Total
Makaton	15	15	14	44
Paget/German			1	1
Bliss Symbolics	1	1	2	4
Combination of more than 1 course	3	2	1	6
No courses	11	11	11	33

While the number of teachers with an initial qualification is high, it falls far short of the 100% which might be expected some thirteen years after the transition of responsibility of special schools from the Department of Health to the D.E.S. However, this is not intended to imply that traditional forms of teacher education, particularly those provided for students wishing to teach in primary schools, are necessarily well suited to the needs of severely mentally handicapped children. On the contrary, there are reasons to suggest that a course which promotes a structured approach emphasising curriculum subjects may be of relatively little value when teachers are confronted by children who need opportunities for language learning. Comparatively few teachers had obtained additional specialist qualifications regarding mentally handicapped children or special education in general.

The length of teaching experience in schools for children with severe and complex learning difficulties also varied from as low as two years to more than twenty years with the highest proportion of teachers having worked in special schools for between five and ten years (Table 3.12).

Table 3.12: Teachers' Experience in Special Schools

Teaching Experience in Years	Pre-verbal	Single Words	Sentences	Total
0 - 2	1	3	3	7
2 - 5	3	6	6	15
5 - 10	14	13	6	33
10 - 15	7	3	7	17
15 - 20	4	1	5	10
20	1	3	2	6
Total	30	29	29	88

Additional Help Within the Classroom

Because of the additional demands in terms of physical care and classroom management made by mentally handicapped children, all of the schools employed additional staff to assist in the classrooms. Depending upon their training and qualifications, these staff members are designated as nursery nurses and teachers' aides or classroom assistants. However, in practice there is little difference in their roles and responsibilities and for the purpose of this discussion the two groups will be considered together. A detailed breakdown of the numbers of nursery nurses, teachers aides and classroom assistants within the 32 schools is shown in Table 3.13.

Table 3.13: Non-Teaching Classroom Staff

	N	Range Within Schools	Mean
Nursery Nurses	179	0(5)* -19	5.78
Nursery Assistants	15	0(27)*- 7	0.48
Teachers' Aides	7	0(28) - 4	0.23
Others	20	0(23) -11	0.64
Total	221	1 -19	
Non-teaching staff pupil ratio 1:25-1:3.4			1:7.8

* No. of schools with no staff in the listed categories.

Looking at the total number of additional classroom staff in relation to the number of pupils in each school the overall ratio is one non-teaching member of staff to approximately 8 children. Thus the distribution of additional staff closely resembles the distribution of teachers within the schools. However, just as the teacher-pupil ratio varied across schools, so the non-teaching staff-pupil ratio varies with some schools having a ratio of 25:1 while others enjoyed one non-teaching staff member for every 3.4 pupils.

Of the teachers who returned questionnaires, all but one had some form of classroom help. Over 87% had at least one full-time nursery nurse although the pre-verbal classes with the younger and often more severely handicapped children tended to have more nursery nurses than the other classes (Table 3.14).

Table 3.14: Distribution of Full-Time Nursery Nurses: Teachers with Different Numbers of Full-Time Nursery Nurses

Number of Nursery Nurses	Pre-verbal		Single Words		Sentences		Total	
	No. of Teachers	No. of Nurses	No. of Teachers	No. of Nurses	No. of Teachers	No. of Nurses	No. of Teachers	No. of Nurses
0	2	0	5	0	4	0	11	0
1	21	21	17	17	23	23	61	61
2	4	8	7	14	2	4	13	26
3	2	6					2	6
4	1	4					1	4
Total	30	39	29	31	29	27	88	97

Table 3.15: Distribution of Part-time Nursery Nurses and Other Types of Classroom Help

	Pre-verbal Help X No. of Classes	Single Words Help X No. of Classes	Sentences Help X No. of Classes	Total Help X No. of Classes	Total F.T. and P.T.
Nursery Nurses P T		1 x 3 = 3	1 x 3 = 3	1 x 6 = 6	6
Assists. F T	1 x 1 = 1 2 x 1 = 2 1 x 1 = 1	1 x 4 = 4	1 x 1 = 1	1 x 6 = 6	10
Assists. P T		1 x 1 = 1	2 x 1 = 2	2 x 2 = 4 1 x 2 = 2	2
YOPS F T	1 x 3 = 3	1 x 1 = 1	1 x 1 = 1	1 x 5 = 5	24
YOPS P T	1 x 5 = 5	1 x 9 = 9	1 x 5 = 5	1 x 19 = 19	
Parents P T	1 x 1 = 1	1 x 1 = 1		1 x 2 = 2	5
Parents F T		3 x 1 = 3		3 x 1 = 3	
Child. P T	1 x 5 = 5	1 x 7 = 7	1 x 4 = 4	1 x 16 = 16	26
Child. F T	2 x 2 = 4	2 x 1 = 2	2 x 2 = 4	2 x 5 = 10	
Total classes and help	19 22	28 31	17 20	64 73	

Approximately 53% of the non-teaching staff (nursery nurses, classroom assistants, teachers' aides) in the schools had a qualification in either child care or education, while just over 13% had been on courses concerned with language and communication during the preceding year. However, once again there was considerable variation across schools with 28 schools having no non-teaching staff who had recently attended courses, and one school having 15. None of those courses issued awards or contributed to a recognised professional qualification.

The Relationship Between the Numbers of Pupils in Schools and the Provision of Teaching and Non-Teaching Staff

Using the index of teachers to pupils and non-teaching staff to pupils, it was possible to examine the relationship between size of schools and the staff-pupil ratio. The correlation co-efficients shown below indicate a statistically significant negative association between school size and staff pupil index for both teachers and non-teaching staff. There is only a moderate and non-significant relationship between numbers of teachers and number of non-teaching staff.

Table 3.16: Pearson Correlation Coefficients: Numbers of Pupils by Pupil-Teacher Ratio and Non-Teaching Staff-Pupil Ratio

	Pupil: teacher ratio	Non-teaching staff: pupil ratio
Number of Pupils in School	$-.59$ $p \leqslant 0.000$	$-.44$ $p \leqslant 0.013$
Non-teaching Staff: Pupil Ratio	$.126$ (N.S.)	

Thus in general, the larger schools had a lower teacher-pupil index than the smaller schools (i.e. more pupils per teacher) and a lower non-teaching staff-pupil index than smaller schools (i.e. more pupils per non-teaching member of staff). This might be expected as a result of economies of scale which would be associated with the larger institutions. However, it raises further questions about the size of classes and the range of handicaps and developmental abilities which might be found in these classes. Is it the case, for example, that the larger schools are able to provide more homogeneous teaching groups which may compensate for the larger class size, while the smaller schools need to have smaller classes since they are more likely to include children with a wide range of abilities and problems? An alternative hypothesis is that size of school and the staff pupil ratios are influenced by different aspects of local authority policy. This question is considered in more detail and in the light of the available evidence below.

Variations in Staff Pupil Ratios Across Local Authorities

In the light of the considerable variation between schools described in the preceding sections, the question arises as to whether such variation is associated with the local authorities which administer the schools. This section, therefore, examines the resources available in the schools in relation to the number of pupils attending the school for the eight local education authorities in Wales.

The number of pupils per school varies considerably with Gwent having an average of over one hundred while the counties of Dyfed, Gwynedd and South Glamorgan have much smaller schools. (It should be noted that two schools in South Glamorgan did not return the questionnaire and therefore a large amount of information for schools in this local authority is not available.) Similarly, there is great variation regarding the number of children attending schools who are either younger than five years of age or older than 16 (Table 3.17). In the counties of Gwent and Powys, there are on average 20 or more of these children per school while in Dyfed the mean figure is as low as 4.5 per school. In general, the local authorities which have large numbers of pupils per school also have the highest numbers of under-fives and pupils over the age of 16 (cf. Gwent, Powys, Mid Glamorgan, West Glamorgan).

Table 3.17: Teaching, Non-teaching and Speech Therapy Provision in Schools for 8 Local Education Authorities (S. = School; P = Pupils; S.T. = Speech Therapy)

Local Authorities	No. of S.	Mean No. of P. per S.	Mean No. of P. +16 yrs.	Mean No. of P. -5 yrs.	Mean No. of P. -5 & +16	Average No. of Pupils per Class	Teacher Pupil Ratio	Non-Teach. Staff Pupil Ratio	Mean % S.T. Time with Pupil Ratio	% Teachers with Initial Qual.	Length of School Day (Mins.)	% Lang. on Time Table
Gwent	3	106	21.3	8	29.3	10.3	1:9.7	1:6.5	.013	63%	301	66%
Powys	1	62	8	12	20	10.33	1:9.1	1:10	.06	57%	315	100%
Mid Glam.	6	84	12.3	5.5	17.8	10.3	1:9.1	1:8.6	.036	86%	312	50%
South Glam.	3	31	5	11	16	7	1:7.0	1:5.1	.04	61%	300	33%
West Glam.	4	54	11	.75	11.75	9.5	1:6.7	1:5.5	.047	78%	293	25%
Dyfed	4	30	3	1.5	4.5	6.5	1:6.5	1:5.3	.08	97%	307	50%
Gwynedd	5	32.4	5.6	2.6	8.2	8.6	1:6.3	1:7.4	.092	82%	302	20%
Clwyd	6	42	6.3	2.1	8.4	8	1:6.8	1:7.9	.028	87%	322	83%

The average number of pupils per class varies from over 10 in three counties to as low as 6.5 and 7 in others, while the teacher-pupil ratio ranges from 1:7 to as high as 1:9. Once again it is the counties with the highest school rolls overall who also have the highest mean teacher-pupil ratios.

The ratio of non-teaching staff to pupils varies from 1:5 in South Glamorgan (again excluding two schools for which no information was available) to 1:10 in Powys. The percentage of teaching staff with an initial teaching qualification is also subject to variation. Three local authorities have a mean of around 60% qualified teachers in their schools, while others have between 80% and 96% qualified staff.

These data strongly suggest that the resources available to schools in relation to their pupil numbers vary considerably from one local authority to another. In particular there is a pattern among some local authorities (Gwent, Powys, Mid Glamorgan and West Glamorgan) of relatively large schools, relatively large numbers of pre-school age and post 16 years pupils, large classes and (except in the case of West Glamorgan) high teacher-pupil ratios.

This pattern is reflected in another way by the correlation coefficients shown in Table 3.16. There is a strong positive correlation between teacher-pupil ratio and size of school. One question which arises from this analysis is the contribution to this pattern made by those pupils who are under age 5 and over age 16. To what extent might local education authority policies and schools policies in relation to these two groups influence the availability of resources for other pupils within the schools?

Re-analysis of some of the data presented in Table 3.17 without the under 5 year old and over 16 year old children is presented in Table 3.18. This shows that without the pre-school age children and post 16 pupils the mean number of pupils per school in all the local authorities falls as does the average number of pupils per class. Similarly, the teacher-pupil ratio falls across the board. This suggests that these pupils are not the main factor contributing to the differential staffing ratios between local authorities. This is confirmed by the fact that when the correlation between school size and teacher-pupil ratio is examined after excluding pre-schoolers and pupils over the age of 16 years the size of the correlation is only slightly reduced and just fails to reach statistical significance (two tailed test; $r = -0.307$; $df = 28$).

Table 3.18: Distribution of Pupils and Teacher-Pupil Ratios Excluding Pupils Under 5 Years and Over 16 Years of Age

	Mean No. of Pupils per School	Mean No. of Pupils per Class	Teacher Pupil Ratio	% of Pre-school and Post-16 Pupils
Gwent	76.6	7.38	1:6.8	28.0
Powys	42	7.00	1:5.9	32.0
Mid Glamorgan	66.1	7.60	1:6.8	25.0
*South Glamorgan	15	3.0	1:0.7	57.0
West Glamorgan	45	8.2	1:4.9	16.25
Dyfed	25.5	5.2	1:3.3	27.75
Gwynedd	21.2	6.3	1:4.6	23.6
Clwyd	33.5	6.37	1:5.4	17.66

* Includes Nursery Unit

However, there is evidence (Table 3.18) of a differential registration of pre-school and post 16 pupils in special schools from one local authority to another. While in Powys (with only one special school) over one-third of the pupils are pre-schoolers or over the age of 16 years, and Gwent, Mid Glamorgan and Dyfed have between 25% and 30% of pupils at these extreme ages, Clwyd and West Glamorgan have only between 16% and 18%. The figure for South Glamorgan is artificially inflated by the non-returns from two schools and the existence of a nursery unit which operates independently and was therefore included as a separate school.

Thus, the overall picture is one of uneven distribution of teaching resources across the eight local education authorities in Wales in relation to children with severe learning difficulties. Some local authorities have higher proportions of children under 5 and over 16 years of age attending schools and this is related to the pattern of resource distribution. Those local authorities with higher school rolls and higher teacher-pupil ratios also have a higher proportion of children below 5 and over 16 years of age. However, this is not the sole cause of this apparent inequality, since differences in numbers of pupils per class and average teacher-pupil ratios remain even when such children are excluded from the analysis (Table 3.18).

SCHOOL ORGANISATION AND TEACHERS' RESPONSIBILITIES

In most special schools children are divided into teaching groups on the basis of age, developmental level or, more usually a combination of factors. The teachers were sampled within the schools on the basis of the head teachers' identification of teaching groups as being mainly at the pre-verbal level, mainly at the single words level, or mainly at the stage of using phrases and sentences. Altogether, 23 teachers identified their teaching groups as 'special care' and a further 3 teachers indicated that some of their children were within this category (Table 3.14). The majority of the special care classes (18) coincided with pre-verbal groups, but there was also one teacher in this category who was identified by the head teacher as working with children who were able to use phrases and sentences.

Table 3.19: Classes Described as Special Care

	Pre-verbal	Single Words	Sentences	Total
Special Care	18	4	1	23
Some Special Care	1	2		3
Not Special Care	10	23	28	61
Total	29*	29	29	87

* Missing data

Table 3.20: Teachers with Special Responsibility for Teaching Language and Communication and Signing or a Symbol System to Children in Other Classes

		Pre-verbal	Single Words	Sentences	Total
	N	30	29	29	88
Language and Communication		5	3	2	10
Signing/ Symbol System		5	5	1	11

Teachers generally considered themselves to be responsible for the organisation of their own classroom areas and the planning of educational activities for their own children. In fourteen of the thirty-two schools sampled, the head teacher reported that one teacher was assigned special responsibility for the teaching of language and communication. Of these, six worked by withdrawing groups of children for special language related activities, three by withdrawing individual children for intensive work, three by working with both groups and individuals and two by working with class teachers. However only eleven teachers saw themselves as responsible for teaching language and communication including sign/symbol systems to children in other classes (Table 3.20). Twelve teachers reported receiving help in language assessment from other members of the school teaching staff. Clearly there is some difference between the head teachers' views of shared responsibility in this area and the extent to which the class teachers feel they have support and assistance from colleagues. In particular, it is noteworthy that the majority of the head teachers who identified staff with special responsibilities in the area of language and communication saw them working directly with children, rather than with their colleagues.

Use of Sign and Symbol Systems Within the Schools

The widespread lack of success in teaching spoken language to mentally handicapped children, and the very slow rates of progress achieved by pupils in special schools in general (Leeming, Swann, Coupe and Mittler, 1979) has led many psychologists and educationalists to advocate training in communication through alternative or augmentative sign or symbol systems.

In a recent study Jones, Reid and Kiernan (1982) found that Makaton vocabulary was by far the most popular signing system within special schools though Kiernan (1984) has also criticised the Makaton system as not being adequately based on research on language development among normal children and for providing only rather general advice on teaching strategies. The most popular symbol system in the Jones et al. study was Bliss which was used in 73.8% of those schools which employed a symbol system. This system involves the user in pointing to a variety of symbols displayed on a rectangular board and although potentially it facilitates greater message complexity, it also has the practical disadvantage of being totally dependent upon the display board. Although the Makaton system is compatible with group work while the Bliss system is better suited to work with individuals, Jones et al. found that nearly 90% of schools employed individual sessions for teaching signs and symbol systems and nearly one third only used individual teaching sessions.

The present study largely corroborated the findings of Jones et al. Altogether 31 of the 32 head teachers indicated use of a non-vocal system in their schools. The most popular system, Makaton, was the only system in use in 19 of the schools, and was used alongside another sign/symbol system in a further 10 schools. The second most popular system was Bliss which was mentioned by 11 head teachers, although in only two of these schools was Bliss the only system used. One school used a system devised by the staff. A similar pattern emerged in respect of the replies from the class teachers; Makaton was the most popular system being cited by 67% of the teachers overall and by over 77% of those teachers who employed some kind of sign/symbol system (see Table 3.21). The next most frequently used system, Bliss, was mentioned by only 15 (17%) of the teachers. Twenty teachers (22%) did not employ any sign or symbol systems.

67

Table 3.21: Frequency of Use of Signing or Symbol Systems

	Pre-verbal	Single Words	Sentences	Total
Makaton	23	20	16	59
Bliss Symbolics	9	1	5	15
Talkmore	0	1	0	1
Own System devised by Teacher and/or Speech Therapist	1	0	2	3
No Signs/Symbol System	3	8	9	20

N = 86

Of the 31 schools which employed a sign/symbol system of some kind, the heads in 30 schools reported that at least one other member of staff was able to use the system. In the one remaining school, the head was the only staff member trained in the use of the sign/symbol system. The number of teachers able to use the sign/symbol system varied from one in one school to twelve in another.

Organisation of the School Day
Using the times provided by the head teachers for the beginning and end of the school day and taking into consideration the time allocated within schools for the lunch break, it was possible to estimate the length of the school day. This varied from 270 minutes (approximately 4 1/2 hours) to 370 minutes (approximately 6 hours) with a mean of 307 minutes (5 hours). Over the course of a week this represents considerable variability with respect to the length of time the children were available for planned educational experiences (see Table 3.17 for the mean length of teaching day across local authorities).

Table 3.22: Teachers' Estimates of Time Spent Per
          Day on Language Lessons

	Pre-verbal	Single Words	Sentences	Total
0-30 minutes	4	7	7	18
31-60 minutes	6	5	11	22
61-120 minutes	10	6	4	20
120-300 minutes	2	4	2	8
N = Missing	8	7	5	20

Organisation of Language Teaching

Whereas only 50% of the head teachers reported that
they required staff to timetable language teaching
periods, 74 teachers (84%) indicated that they set
aside particular periods during the week for
teaching language skills. The teachers who did set
aside language teaching periods were then asked to
give details about the organisation and content of
these lessons (see Chapter 5). On average, teachers
estimated that the time spent per day on activities
specifically directed at encouraging language was 78
minutes although this varied from a low of 10
minutes to a high of 300 minutes, i.e. the whole day
(Table 3.22). There is no evidence of differential
allocation of time according to overall language
level of the children in a class. It should also be
mentioned that many teachers, including some of
those who completed this item, added that language
teaching was not something which is restricted to
timetabled activities but also permeates many other
activities during the school day. In response to a
questionnaire item which specifically asked teachers
to indicate how much opportunity their children had
for practising language skills outside language
teaching periods, 76 (86%) indicated 'numerous
opportunities', 3 'some opportunities' and only 2
said that there was little opportunity for language
learning during the rest of the school day.

The data presented in Table 3.22 is therefore
difficult to interpret since the estimate of time
spent on working specifically on language skills is
confounded by the different ways in which teachers
might interpret their activities with the children.
Similar activities might be conducted with different
aims. For example, is using Lego an activity

focussed on manipulative skills, perceptual abilities, problem solving or social and communicative skills? It could of course be intended to facilitate development in all these areas. Inclusion of specific activities when the teachers responded to this item would depend upon their perception of that situation. It would also depend upon the teacher's interpretation of the question and the phrase 'working specially on language skills' does not specifically preclude activities which are set up with a number of different developmental aims in mind. Table 3.22 therefore may be interpreted as showing <u>either</u> a high degree of variation with regard to the amount of time teachers spend on language related activities <u>or</u> a highly varied interpretation of what constitutes a language related activity or a combination of both these factors. For clarification, this requires a more detailed examination of teachers' views of language and language learning activities, using the more sensitive interviewing techniques. This is the subject of a related study which will be reported separately.

SUMMARY

This chapter has represented quantitative data from the schools involved in this study regarding the pupils, teachers and other staff and general organisational characteristics of the schools. The schools in general are not large, with the majority having somewhere between 50 and 100 pupils and between 5 and 7 classes. The classes vary in size, but most have between six and ten children. The majority of the pupils are regarded by both head teachers and class teachers as being primarily mentally handicapped although a relatively high proportion have at least one additionally handicapping condition. The ages of the pupils within schools and within classes vary considerably since the main criteria of establishing teaching groups are ability and developmental status.

The majority of the teaching staff (although by no means all) are qualified teachers, but only about half of those sampled had specialist qualifications concerned with the care and education of mentally handicapped children. Nearly two-thirds had been on courses concerned with sign or symbol systems for augmenting spoken language. Nearly all of the teachers had additional full-time help within the classroom and about half of these non-teaching staff members had appropriate child care qualifications. In general, there was strong evidence that the larger schools employed higher staff pupil ratios than the smaller schools, although this was confounded to some extent by considerable variations across local authorities, particularly in respect to the proportion of very young and post 16 year pupils who attended the schools. Although the teachers were pre-selected as working with children at three levels of linguistic ability (pre-verbal, single words, phrases and sentences) about 24% identified the children in their classes as 'special care'. Although about half of the head teachers (N = 32) indicated that there was one member of staff with overall responsibility for language and communication within the school, only 11 of the teachers saw themselves as having this responsibility and only 12 reported receiving help in language assessment from another member of staff. For the majority of schools staff responsibility for language and communication across the school involved withdrawing children from other classes for intensive work, rather than working with other members of staff. Makaton vocabulary and/or Bliss symbols were used in many schools and in nearly all of the schools at least one member of staff other than the head was experienced in the classroom use of one of the systems.

The schools day varied from about 4 1/2 to about 6 hours. Whereas only 50% of the head teachers indicated that they liked language and communication activities to be formally recognised within a class timetable, over 80% of the teachers said that they set aside particular periods within the week for teaching language skills. Teacher estimates of amount of time per day spent on language related activities varied from as little as 10 minutes to virtually the whole day.

Chapter Four

THE AIMS AND METHODS OF LANGUAGE ASSESSMENT

This chapter deals with the teachers' approach to
the assessment of linguistic abilities among the
mentally handicapped pupils in their classes. It
begins with a consideration of the purpose of
linguistic assessments from the teachers' point of
view, before describing the frequency and methods
for assessment currently in use in the classrooms.

TEACHERS' VIEWS ON LANGUAGE ASSESSMENT

Teachers' views on assessment were examined by
providing five statements describing different aims
of language assessments and inviting teachers to
rank them in order of importance. This rather
artificial device was included because it was felt
that if teachers were simply required to rate the
items individually as being important or
unimportant, there was a strong possibility that
they would all be rated as very important. The item
is artificial because there is no necessary
contradiction between the different aims of
assessment and all might be regarded as valid. On
the other hand, this item does force the respondents
to differentiate between different aims and in doing
so it is suggested that it provides an indication of
underlying attitudes towards assessment.

Table 4.1 shows how the teachers ranked the
five items and the mean rank for each item. The data
were examined for congruity with regard to teachers'
rating of the five items using Kendall's coefficient
of concordance (W) (Siegel, 1956). This produced a W
= 0.4589 (4df) significant beyond $p \leqslant 0.0001$ showing a
high degree of consistency within this group of
teachers. The item most consistently ranked highest
was 'to provide a basis for planning relevant

teaching objectives' (mean rank 1.7) while items concerned with 'understanding the child' and monitoring progress were second and third most popular with mean ranks of 2.65 and 2.74 respectively. In contrast, the least popular items were 'to provide the teacher with information so that he/she can talk knowledgeably about the child to other teachers, professionals and parents' (mean rank 4.7) and 'to help the teacher to assess the effectiveness of teaching' (mean rank 3.13). Taken together these data suggest that the teachers gave higher rankings to those items which presented assessment as an activity conducted in relation to the child, and gave lower priority to items in which assessment was related to communication among professionals and to teacher effectiveness.

The low ranking of assessment for communication with other teachers, professionals and parents is consistent with special school teachers having (and possibly desiring) relatively little contact with other professionals and parents. The relatively low rank ascribed to assessment for ascertaining teacher effectiveness may be indicative of a particular theoretical and ideological standpoint in which language is seen as a skill possessed by the child and influenced by intra-individual variation among pupils, rather than an interpersonal skill which is closely related to the strategies employed by linguistically more competent conversational partners - in this case teachers. Similarly assessment may be regarded as an activity which is performed by teachers on pupils with relatively little attention given to the interdependent relationship between the child's and teacher's language.

FREQUENCY OF LANGUAGE ASSESSMENTS

The teachers were asked a number of questions concerned with their classroom practices for language assessment. The first of these was 'How often do you normally make a written assessment of

Table 4.1:   Rank   Ordering by Teachers of Five
             Statements Regarding the Purpose of
             Language Assessments

Items	Ranking					Mean Rank
	1	2	3	4	5	
To provide a basis for planning teaching objectives	44	23	10	6	1	1.7
To help the teacher understand the child better	19	23	14	24	4	2.65
To enable the teacher to monitor the child's progress	14	17	31	21	1	2.74
To help the teacher assess the effectiveness of teaching	7	19	23	26	9	3.13
To provide the teacher with information so that she/he can talk knowledgeably about the child to other teachers, professionals and parents	0	3	5	6	70	4.7

Kendall Coefficient of Concordance = .4589, df = 4,
p ≤ 0.0001, N = 84

the language and communication skills of the
children in your class?' The responses to this
question are summarised in Table 4.2. Over 20% of
the teachers made written assessments of language
and communication once a year or less, while a
further 58% of the teachers did so about once every
term. Only 22% of the teachers reported making such
assessments at least once per week. The pattern
across the class categories is very similar, with
the mode in each case being once per term.

Table 4.2:   Frequency of Written Assessments of
             Language and Communication Skills

	Pre-verbal	Single Words	Sentences	Total
Seldom if at all		1	1	2
About once a year	4	5	7	16
About once per term	18	15	18	51
At least once per week	8	8	3	19

AVAILABILITY OF WRITTEN ASSESSMENTS

All the teachers indicated that their written
assessments were made available to other people.
They were then asked to indicate 'who would normally
see your assessment?' The responses to this question
are summarised in Table 4.3. Over 80% of the
teachers indicated that their head teacher would
normally see their assessments and almost as many
made them available to the non-teaching staff in
their classrooms. Three-quarters of the teachers
shared their assessments with other professionals
such as speech therapists. On the other hand, only
about half of the teachers and in the case of the
pre-verbal classes only 37% normally made their
assessments available to parents. This is consistent
with the views expressed by head teachers regarding
co-operation with parents described in Chapter Six.

Table 4.3: Availability of Written Assessments to Other Professionals and Parents

	Pre-verbal		Single Words		Sentences		Total	
		%		%		%		%
Non-teaching staff in class room	25	83	21	72	25	86	71	81
Other teachers	14	47	17	59	16	55	47	53
Headteachers	24	80	24	83	26	90	74	84
Child's Parents	11	37	18	62	12	41	41	47
Other Professionals	23	77	20	69	23	79	66	75
Local Authority Advisers	10	33	10	34	8	28	28	32
Others	4	13	4	14	0	0	4	5

N =   30   29   29   88

% rounded to nearest whole number

METHODS OF ASSESSMENT

The teachers were then asked to indicate using a simple three point scale how often they used different language assessment instruments. Many of the instruments listed in the questionnaire were taken from a report of a previous study concerned with developmental assessment by teachers in special schools (Gibbs, 1982) although a number of items specifically concerned with the assessment of language and communication were added. For all classes, irrespective of language level, Table 4.4 shows that the most popular assessment instruments were the Gunzberg Progress Assessment Charts (Gunzberg, 1973), mentioned by 57% of the teachers, and the Portage Checklist (Shearer and Shearer, 1976), mentioned by 64% of the teachers. Both of these scales include language abilities within a wider ranging list of developmentally sequenced abilities and, perhaps because of this, the language assessments which can be derived from these instruments are relatively crude.

Furthermore, Portage is essentially a highly structured programme for intervention with respect to a number of developmental areas such as communication and self help. As might be expected the high frequency of use of Portage for assessment purposes was coupled with frequent use of the Portage teaching scheme. However, whereas 64% of the teachers indicated that Portage was used for assessment purposes, only 42% mentioned Portage in connection with teaching language (see Chapter Five below).

Table 4.4: Instruments Used in Classroom Assessments of Language and Communication

	Pre-verbal		Single Words		Sentences		Total	
	F	S	F	S	F	S	F	S
Sheridan Scales	0	3	0	0	2	0	2	3
Scales from Derbyshire Language Scheme	2	0	1	0	1	3	4	3
Reynell Language Development Scales	1	7	4	4	2	4	7	15
Hester Adrian Language Charts	0	5	3	1	1	2	4	8
Language Charts from 'Let me Speak'	3	3	2	1	0	4	5	8
Gunzberg Progress Assessment Charts	9	8	11	6	12	4	32	18
Portage Checklist	16	8	14	5	10	3	40	16
National Children's Bureau Dev. Guide	1	2	0	2	0	1	1	5
Teachers' Develop. Assessment Charts	3	0	3	2	2	1	6	3
L.A.R.S.P.	2	1	1	1	2	2	5	4
D.I.S.T.A.R.	0	1	1	1	1	1	2	3
Others	0	6	0	8	0	5	0	19

F = frequently: S = sometimes

Approximately 25% of the teachers used the Reynell Developmental Language Scales (Reynell, 1969), but only 8% did so frequently. The Language Development Charts from 'Let Me Speak' (Jeffree and McConkey, 1976) were used by 15% of the teachers, while the Hester Adrian Language Charts (Cunningham and Jeffree, 1971) were referred to by 14% of the teachers. Overall 74% of the teachers referred to more than one instrument for making assessments of children's language and communication, 23% referred to only one instrument while 3.5% used no formal procedure. (Of the three teachers who did not refer to formal assessment instruments, two were in classes with children using phrases and sentences and one was in a class with children using mainly single words.)

In response to a question on whether there were 'any other methods you would normally use to monitor the language and communication skills of the children in your class?', a total of 39 teachers (44%) provided descriptions of additional procedures. The most frequently cited comments (9) referred to the use of additional, often specially designed, checklists or systems for profiling the development of individual children. Seven teachers referred to observing the children informally in relatively naturalistic settings and six specifically made reference to writing down what the children said. The same number commented on the use of audio and video recorders to assist in the process of observation. Seven teachers mentioned assessing progress in relation to the success with which they were able to teach behaviourally defined objectives (e.g. 'weekly percentage scores of programme work plotted on a graph') and a further five described different kinds of activity which were specifically designed to assist in the process of assessment (e.g. 'pictures to monitor the construction of sentences' - presumably referring to a commercially produced set of cards). There was little difference in terms of the proportion of teachers from each of the three class categories who made comments regarding additional forms of assessment and little indication that the teachers introduced different assessment procedures in response to the language levels of the children in their classes. The only suggestion of such a tendency was that whereas seven teachers of pre-verbal children referred to the Makaton Vocabulary as providing a useful form of assessment, only one other teacher from the other two categories did so.

SUMMARY

Teachers' views of language assessment emphasised the role of assessments in planning teaching exercises. Relatively low priority was given to formal assessments as way of obtaining information which could be communicated to other professionals and parents and as a way of assessing teaching effectiveness. The majority of teachers made written assessments of the children very infrequently. Only 22% reported making assessments at least once per week with the others reporting assessments as taking place once per term or less frequently. In general, assessments were made available to the head teacher, other class teachers in the school and relevant professionals such as speech therapists. However, only 47% of teachers normally made assessments available to parents. No information is available regarding to what extent such availability resulted in parents reading the assessments and discussing them with the teachers.

The most frequently used assessment instruments were general scales or developmental charts (e.g. Portage, Gunzberg Progress Assessment Charts) which included specific language items. These instruments generally rely upon the teacher's evaluation of whether or not a child employs a specific linguistic structure or function in specified settings. They do not provide test data in the sense of indicating what a child <u>can</u> do under specified conditions; rather they summarise certain factors of the child's communicative abilities observed in daily classroom activities. Although the summarising and recording may be useful, these charts and scales by their very nature are unlikely to provide the teacher with any new information regarding a child's linguistic ability. They may however introduce the teacher to new terminology or to different ways of thinking about language development.

In addition to commercially available instruments, many teachers (44%) employed additional procedures including their own specially designed checklists, notes based on observation, and the use of audio and video recordings. This suggests that for a large number of teachers, the commercial assessment instruments were either not available, or did not fulfil their needs in terms of classroom based assessments.

Chapter Five

STRATEGIES FOR LANGUAGE TEACHING

This chapter looks at organisational aspects of language teaching such as the size of groups teachers preferred to work with and the choice of materials employed in these sessions. It also presents descriptive data based on teachers' accounts of the kinds of activity they tried to initiate among the children as a basis for language learning. Descriptions of actual activities are compared with descriptions produced in response to a questionnaire item which asked teachers to describe 'the single most important thing you can do to encourage language and communication skills'. It is suggested that the different types of response reflect the conflict between an educational ideology with focusses on didactic teaching skills and a developmental ethos which emphasises open ended 'playful' activities leading to productive but unpredictable outcomes.

Before going on to detailed questions about language teaching in the classroom, the teachers were asked to indicate how important they regarded language development in relation to other kinds of activity that might be encouraged in the classroom. This item was considered necessary to avoid possible ambiguity in relation to the responses to subsequent items. After all, if some teachers regarded language learning as a low priority for their children, it would be unreasonable to compare their language related classroom practices with those teachers who placed a high priority on language development. On a scale ranging from 'very important' through 'of some importance' and 'not very important' to 'of no importance', 80 teachers (91%) rated language as very important and 8 teachers (9%) rated it as 'of some importance'. This indicates a strong consensus regarding the value attached to language learning by teachers of children with severe learning difficulties. The rest of this book is concerned with the variations which were reported regarding the way in which teachers organise classroom activities to promote language learning, a description of the help techers received from outside the school, and a summary of the comments made by head teachers and class teachers regarding improving the quality of language teaching in special schools.

THE SIZE OF TEACHING GROUPS

In order to examine preferences for different types of classroom organisation the teachers were asked to indicate the relative frequency with which they taught the whole class, small groups or individuals when working on language and communication skills. Table 5.1 shows the percentages of teachers' responses for different size groups across the three levels of language ability.

A number of trends are evident within this Table. First, whereas overall, the main response category for whole class and small groups is 'sometimes' the main response category for singles is 'usually' (66%). Furthermore, over 25% of teachers 'hardly ever' use the whole class. The figure for the 'hardly ever' category falls to 8.6% for small groups and there are no teachers who responded 'hardly ever' to singles teaching.

Secondly, within this general pattern of responses there are clear trends for teachers working with children of different ability levels. Consider first the teachers working mainly with pre-verbal children. Over 45% 'hardly ever' work with the whole class while about 50% work with the whole class 'sometimes'. Small groups are more popular, with nearly 56% choosing this form of grouping 'sometimes', 29% using groups 'usually' and only 25% 'hardly ever'. For singles the trend continues with 88% of these teachers usually working with individual children and 12% working with individuals sometimes. Teachers of children with single words show a slightly different response pattern with more choosing whole class teaching 'usually' (27%) and 'sometimes' (54%) and correspondingly fewer responding 'hardly ever'. Small groups are more popular with those teachers with 73% indicating that they are 'sometimes' used and none indicating

Table 5.1: Teachers' Preferences for Size of Teaching Groups

	Usually				Sometimes				Hardly Ever			
	PV%	SW%	SENT%	X̄	PV%	SW%	SENT%	X̄	PV%	SW%	SENT%	X̄
Whole Class N = 77	12.5	29.1	21.7	20.8	41.6	54.1	56.5	51.4	45.8	16.6	21.7	27
Small Group N = 70	29.1	26	52	35.7	45.8	73	48	55.7	25	0	0	8.6
Single Pupils N = 77	88	64	46	66	12	36	54	33.8	0	0	0	0

PV – Teachers working with pre-verbal pupils
SW – Teachers working with pupils using mainly single words
SENT – Teachers working with pupils using mainly phrases and sentences

Rows PV, SW and Sentences sum to 100%

Slight deviations from 100% are due to rounding of %

'hardly ever'. Again singles are the most popular with 64% of teachers indicating that they usually employ one-to-one teaching for language and communication and the remaining 36% opting for singles 'sometimes'. For teachers of children using mainly phrases and sentences 56% sometimes taught the whole class, and 21% usually. However, small groups were more frequently employed than either the whole class or singles. Fifty-two per cent of those teachers 'usually' worked with small groups and 48% 'sometimes' worked with small groups. This pattern was reversed in the case of singles with only 46% 'usually' opting for one-to-one teaching and 54% choosing one-to-one 'sometimes'.

To summarise these trends, it appears that most teachers favour one-to-one teaching over whole class and small group teaching. This pattern is most noticeable with teachers of children who have little or no spoken language and slightly less marked with teachers of children using single words. For teachers with children using sentences and phrases small groups are preferred to both singles and whole class teaching. Thus there is a positive association between linguistic level of pupils and preferred size of teaching groups. Teachers with more able pupils (in terms of language) are more likely to prefer group teaching and less likely to indicate a strong preference for one-to-one teaching. This trend invites further investigation in terms of how it relates to teachers' perceptions. Specifically, it suggests a view of language acquisition and language teaching which is highly dependent upon one-to-one teaching in the early stages, but less so as children's mastery of language develops. There is no evidence that class size per se is related to choice of classroom organisation for language teaching (see Table 3.1) although it is possible that developmental characteristics of the children, for example distractability, play some part in the teachers decisions regarding classroom organisation. Similarly, it is difficult to find any variation in the distribution of non-teaching classroom staff which might be associated with the trends described for organisation during languge teaching sessions (see Tables 3.14 and 3.15).

MATERIALS AND TEACHING KITS

The use of commercially produced teaching kits which focus, at least in part, on language development, is shown in Table 5.2. As was the case with the frequency of use of assessment instruments (see Table 4.4) the Portage guide (Shearer and Shearer, 1976) is the most popular, being used by 42% of the teachers. Other programmes were much less popular with Jim's People (Thomas, Gaskin and Herriot, 1978) being used by nearly 15% of the teachers and each of the others being used by 10% or less. Sixteen teachers did not use any of the commercial language teaching programmes. Since the Portage scheme is designed as a general developmental programme which is not directed specifically at language, these data may give an inflated estimate of the extent to which teachers are employing programmes for language teaching.

Table 5.2: Teachers' Use of Language Teaching Programmes (N = 86)

	Pre-verbal	Single Words	Sentences	Total
Portage	19	9	9	37
Let Me Speak	3	1	1	5
Gillham's First Words Programme	3	3	0	6
Derbyshire Language Scheme	2	2	3	7
L.A.R.S.P.	3	3	2	8
D.I.S.T.A.R.	1	2	0	3
Jim's People	3	6	4	13
Peabody	1	2	2	5
Language Master Programme	1	0	0	1
Goal	2	0	1	3
Talkmore	0	1	1	2
Holt Pre-Reading	1	0	0	1
Material prepared by Speech Therapist/ Teacher	1	1	2	4
None	6	5	5	16

N=30   N=27   N=26

23 Teachers reported using more than one of the above programmes.

In addition to language programmes, the teachers were asked to describe other materials used during language teaching sessions. These are shown in Table 5.3. The most popular items were picture books mentioned by over 80% of the teachers, toys 68%, and puzzles 60%. In response to a request for more detailed information 40 teachers provided lists of the toys they normally used during language teaching sessions (Table 5.4). These roughly divide into symbolic toys (including dolls, puppets, model animals, cars, tea sets, etc.) activity toys (such as balls, sand, water, crayons), pictures and real objects. By far the most frequently cited materials were symbolic toys or models of real objects, people and animals.

Table 5.3: Materials Used by Teachers in Language Periods (N = 74)

	Pre-verbal	Single Words	Sentences	Total
Toys	22	22	16	60
Picture Books	23	25	24	72
Puzzles	16	21	16	53
Television/Video-recorder	9	15	16	40
Audio Tape Recorder	14	13	17	44
Lanuage Master	3	6	13	22
Micro-Computer	0	0	4	4
OHP - Film/Slide Projector	0	1	1	2
No response	4	3	2	9

Table 5.4: Toys Mentioned in Relation to Language Teaching (N = 40)

	Pre-verbal	Single Words	Sentences	Total
Dolls, teddies, etc.	8	2	5	15
Puppets	8	6	6	12
Model animals/farm animals	5	3	1	9
Model people	3	1	1	5
Model cars	7	5	3	15
Tea set/dolls' furniture	3		2	5
Miscellaneous Models	2			2
Wendy House, dolls house	3	5	4	12
Cot,pram	1			1
Bricks, blocks	3	1	1	5
Ball	3			3
Sand, water	3			3
Crayons, paints	2			2
Pictures/photos	6			6
Real objects (cup, spoon, etc.)	3			3
Mirror		1		1
Dressing up		1		1
Telephone			1	1

TEACHING ACTIVITIES

Although there are obvious disadvantages and considerable limitations to a procedure which requires respondents to reflect on and then describe their own activity, it was considered that a question about the nature of teaching activities was desirable within this questionnaire. Thus, those teachers who indicated that they did set aside particular periods for language teaching activities, were asked to describe 'the sorts of activity you would normally include in periods devoted to encouraging language development'. It was also suggested that 'it may help to focus on the things you do with one specific child'. Overall, 73 teachers provided brief descriptions of classroom

activities. From these desciptions, a number of
categories were generated, and the number of
teachers who mentioned each type of activity is
shown in Table 5.5. These categories are to some
extent artificial and there is some degree of
overlap between them. For example, naming is an
activity which is often associated with looking at
picture books but is not necessarily or exclusively
attached to picture books.

Table 5.5: Descriptions of Language Teaching
Activities (Only categories receiving
5 or more mentions overall N = 73)

	Pre-verbal	Single Words	Sentences	Total
Looking at picture books	8	13	12	33
*Naming activities (recognition of object names, naming objects, naming actions)	7	9	7	23
Singing, drama, physical games	11	8	7	26
Table games	5	2	2	9
Dolls, puppets, symbolic play	5	6	4	15
Class discussion. 'News' periods	1	4	8	13
Stories	3	5	2	10
*Listening skills	3	3	5	11
*Body awareness	3	2	0	5
*Vocalisation/ specific sounds	5	3	0	8
Matching, sorting	5	0	2	7
*Linguistic/ grammatical categories	2	7	4	13
Reading, pre-reading activities	2	1	2	5
Concepts, sequencing, classification	2	3	3	8
Visits/shopping	1	2	3	6

* Items which identify teaching goals

Since the categories in Table 5.5 were generated from the teachers' own descriptions, they provide an indication of the different perspectives employed for viewing language teaching. Just as pictures and picture books were among the most popular materials, so looking at pictures and picture books feature as the most popular activities carried out in relation to language teaching. While looking at picture books received the highest number of mentions from teachers working with children able to use single words or phrases, for teachers working with less able children, looking at picture books took second place to singing, drama and 'body' games.

Naming pictures, objects or actions was, overall, the second most frequently mentioned activity. The way in which pictures and picture books were used to encourage familiarity with objects, activities and associated verbal labels can be seen from the quotations which follow. The popularity of picture books and naming activities is presumably closely related to the teachers perceptions of what constitutes an appropriate activity for language learning, and the effectiveness of this material is likely to be dependent upon how it is used. However, at this stage, it is possible to speculate that, as with adults interacting with normal (non-handicapped) children, picture books facilitate the negotiation of joint reference. They may enable the teacher to predict and to some extent control the experiences to which the child's language relates. In this way the use of picture books may enhance the teacher's capacity to manage and monitor the immediate communicative context. This is likely to have two advantages. First, it increases the liklihood that the teacher's utterances will be identified with a specific perceptual array. For example, the teacher may feel that looking at a picture book will increase the chances of demonstrating word reference where the activity involves naming a class of objects (e.g. dog) while the child is looking at a picture which exemplifies that class of objects in some way (e.g. a picture of a retriever). Secondly, the controlled context of picture books presumably places considerable constraints on the meanings which are likely to be expressed by the children. Utterances may not be wholly predictable, but the teacher may feel considerably more confident in offering interpretations within a situation whereby conversational topics are generally derived from or at least related to, the material in the picture.

Set against these advantages are a number of possible disadvantages. First, since topics for conversation between the teacher and the child are constrained by the pictures on each page, there is less chance of the child becoming interested in the activity. In fact, for some children the necessity of dealing with pictorial representations of real objects may raise problems of its own. Secondly, unless the pictures are particularly well chosen they may not reflect the child's own experiences, and therefore may be difficult to interpret. Finally, looking at a picture book severely restricts the kinds of social interaction which can occur and for this reason it lacks the flexibility of some other activities.

Whether or not such a strategy is indeed effective in assisting language learning for mentally handicapped children requires empirical data which are not currently available. However, once again it is possible to speculate that effectiveness would be associated with the existing linguistic abilities of the child, and the way in which such picture book activities were integrated with other language learning experiences.

Apart from 'naming' and 'recognition' of objects and activities the only other descriptions which presupposed a level of linguistic or grammatical analysis by the teacher was 'use of prepositions' (9 mentions), verbs (3 mentions), nouns (1 mention), pronouns (1 mention) and activities designed to elicit labial plosives ('p' and 'b'; 4 mentions). Three other categories are concerned with teaching objectives associated with linguistic ability; body awareness (5 mentions), listening skills (11 mentions) and vocalisations (4 mentions). (N.B. in Table 5.6 activities designed to elicit plosives and non-specific vocalisations are collapsed into one category.) All other comments were descriptions of activities, which presumably were regarded as being likely to enhance language use or language comprehension by the children.

All of these descriptions represent variations on traditional didactic exchanges in which the teacher selects <u>something</u> and some activity to be the focus of attention for adult and child and thus to provide the referential meaning for the language to be learned. The teachers seem to be thinking about language as a curriculum subject which is best dealt with through the application of traditional teaching methods. There is a noticeable absence of descriptions of activities or social routines specifically concerned with stimulating naturalistic communicative interactions. There would seem to be little opportunity for spontaneous child-initiated communication unless this is closely related to the stimulus materials.

TEACHERS' DESCRIPTIONS OF LANGUAGE RELATED ACTIVITIES

This section presents examples of the teachers' descriptions of classroom activities designed to encourage language and communication.

Teachers Working with Pre-verbal Children

Makaton sessions every day; play sessions every day in Wendy house. Use of songs to learn everyday phrases; games to encourage vocalisation. Careful use of speech at all times.

Symbolic play - from concrete to imaginative; movement and body awareness - naming body parts; object to picture - picture to picture. Specific recognition of common objects - concept formation - development of use of prepositions.

Asking the child to name various objects, to match pairs of pictures, to join in simple nursery rhymes and songs, to name and point to parts of the body. Use of form boards with simple everyday objects depicted.

Teachers Working with Children Using Mainly Single Words

Music and movement, body awareness, body parts. Spatial concepts; symbolic play - large toys - symbolic play; small items - objects and pictures; pictures and pictures. Recognition of everyday objects - concept formation.

Group 'chat' sessions. Individual work with pictures, etc. group work choosing one particular area (e.g. prepositions) children providing reinforcement for each other. Stories - again taking one area of language for each child, i.e. knowing stage of each child.

Teachers Working with Children Able to Use Sentences

Every advantage is taken to involve as much oral work as possible. Children encouraged to tell own news and talk about various objects of interest, etc. They are involved in a very limited amount of written work and one can read quite fluently. Vast use is made of language self-corrective work boxes, lotto games, etc. Always aware that emphasis is put on acceptable oral work in every activity.

Using large floor puzzle of an adventure playground encourage 3-4 word sentences by asking specific questions, e.g. 'Is the boy on the swing or on the slide?' Answer - 'the boy is on the slide'. 'How many children are in the pool?' 'Where would you like to play?'

As can be seen from Table 5.5 and from the brief selection of quotations, teachers interpreted the question about language teaching activities in two ways; one interpretation concerned the kinds of linguistic activity which the child needed to demonstrate - naming, practising specific sounds - and the other interpretation gave rise to descriptions of the kinds of adult-child activity which might provide an appropriate setting for the rehearsal of such linguistic skills. Needless to say, it was relatively unusual for teachers to state both the adult-child teaching activity, _and_ the particular linguistic skill which it was supposed to elicit. However, the distinction is a very important one within the classroom and it runs parallel to an important theoretical debate within developmental psychology. In essence, this debate concerns the relationship between behaviours which are indicative of developmental progress (naming, symbolic play, etc.), the psychological processes and mental structures which underly such behaviours, and the social interactions between children and adults (or children and their peers) which provide a context for the meaningful elaboration of behaviour and hence the development of understanding.

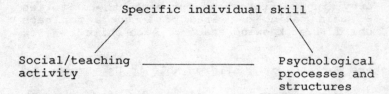

Specific individual skill

Social/teaching activity ————————— Psychological processes and structures

This diagram indicates the inter-relationships between these three aspects of intelligent behaviour. Social or teaching activities depend upon the teacher engaging the child in some form of communicative routine; and in order to do this the teacher must exploit what might be regarded as individual skills - the kinds of things that the child can do. These social/teaching activities then provide the context for the elaboration of underlying 'meaning structures' such that the child is able to extend his or her repertoire of individual skills. This may take the form of endowing existing skills with a deeper significance so that, for example, 'fingering' objects becomes 'pointing' in an expressive or communicative sense. Alternatively, it may provide opportunities for the child to realise and express existing ways of understanding through conventional or semi-conventional vocal means or through signing.

While this triangular set of relations provides a useful framework for discussing the respective contributions of teacher and child in specific teaching activities, it is but a part of a wider social context which frames the meaning of the teaching activity itself. And just as the classroom and the special school provide an institutional context for this kind of teaching, so the educational system and the wider social and cultural environment provide a context for special schools. Thus, the meaning of the linguistic exchanges which occur between teacher and child depend upon various interdependent levels of context (Hinde, 1986; Markova, 1986 and Chapter Two). This theoretical point has considerable practical significance for two reasons. First, it suggests that the way in which the teaching context is interpreted will place considerable constraints on the meanings which a child can express. Didactic strategies make available different meanings in comparison to more open-ended process oriented strategies. Secondly, the introduction of curriculum innovations which challenge traditional views of teaching, require that teachers (who inevitably control the selection of teaching activities) must be encouraged to reconsider the practices associated with the contexts of schools and classrooms; specifically they need to understand that language facilitation may be accomplished by methods other than direct instruction.

The descriptions of teaching activities provided by the teachers included all three elements in the triangular relationship. However, from the point of view of deliberate intervention, there are three important limitations in those descriptions. The first is the lack of detailed description of appropriate individual skills, social activities or psychological processes. The second limitation is that the teachers' comments seldom linked the different descriptions explicitly in terms of social activities, the child's contribution to those activities and what the child might be expected to learn as a result of his/her participation. The third aspect of these comments is that, with few exceptions, they place very little emphasis on conversational aspects of language (McTear, 1985, Ochs and Schieffelin, 1979, 1983). References to language are almost solely in terms of naming, recognition, listening, learning grammatical categories or phonological distinctions. Language is referred to in terms of discrete cognitive skills to be demonstrated by the individual child in structured activities.

Interestingly, very different descriptions of children's language were given in response to another question which asked 'What do you feel is the single most important thing you can do to encourage the development of language and communication skills in the children you work with?' This question gave rise to a range of comments which are summarised in Table 5.6. These comments show a much greater emphasis on the teacher understanding the child and being understood as a conversational partner by the child than was the case when the teachers were simply asked to describe the teaching activities they established in the classroom. For example, one teacher who worked mainly with pre-verbal children commented 'develop child's self awareness and get him motivated to use words, i.e. to express themselves and to develop a naturalness when they communicate with others'. There was also a greater awareness shown of the value of language in the everyday lives of the children. Another teacher working with pre-verbal children suggested 'to help each other with everyday tasks and to integrate as

93

often as possible with other children and adults in as many normal situations as possible, e.g. going to the shop, P.O., etc., dining with normal children and visiting cafes.' Yet another teacher of pre-verbal children commented 'to keep language at a level at which they can understand and to make an attempt to understand them no matter how they are communicating.'

Teachers with more able children made similar comments. For example, four teachers who worked with children using single words commented: 'converse meaningfully and simply with the children throughout the day and encouraging a response be it verbal or non-verbal', 'provide a stimulating and motivating environment which stimulates the children to feel the need to communicate', 'communicating with children at all times - whatever the activity','talk to the children and encourage them to respond'.

Finally, three teachers with more able children using phrases and sentences, made the following comments: 'create situations where language frequently becomes essential, not only to one adult, but with other children and adults in school and outside school','talking to the children in a way which encourages children to respond in longer phrases and sentences', 'talk to the children at every opportunity and give each child the chance to express him/herself regardless of speech skills'.

This final quotation nicely emphasises the distinction which was apparent from many of the comments made in response to, on the one hand a question about teaching activities and, on the other, a question about the most important things a teacher could do. While the former question was answered in terms of individual skills which demonstrated discrete aspects of linguistic functioning, the latter question was answered in terms of communication, conversations, understanding and using language in naturalistic contexts. This difference provides a clear indication that the kinds of activity which teachers promote when teaching language in timetabled periods are not the activities which they consider to be most relevant to the development of language and communication skills. One might then ask why they continue with those activities described as occurring within the timetabled periods. Although this questionnaire did not tackle this issue directly, it is possible to speculate that the ideology of instruction associated with being a teacher in a school, and the considerable administrative and organisational constraints influence teachers activities, at least as much as intuitions about 'good practice' (see Harris, 1985).

Table 5.6: Descriptions of 'Single Most Important Thing to Encourage Children's Language and Communication' (N = 80, figures refer to number of teachers citing each item)

Type of Comment	Pre-verbal	Single Words	Sentences	Total
Structured teaching and specific objectives	3	3	1	7
Stimulate child	1	6	1	8
Talk to the child	8	7	4	19
Listen to the child - try to understand	4	3	5	12
Simplified adult language	1	0	1	2
Emphasise correct speech	0	2	2	4
Motivate the child, give the child confidence, establish a good relationship	4	6	3	13
Encourage linguistic communication	7	9	9	25
Build on every day experiences	2	0	1	3
Emphasise one-to-one teaching	3	1	2	6
Encourage talk with peers	0	1	3	4
Encourage play	0	0	2	2

Teaching a child to say certain words in response to specific pictorial configurations in a picture book can be recognised as an explicitly pedagogical activity. The teacher is able to identify certain skills which the child is unable to demonstrate. By engaging the child in an activity which employs demonstration, imitation, repetition and encouragement, the teacher may be able to teach the child those specific skills and to monitor the child's progress over a period of days or weeks. Moreover, this is a strategy which has been widely advocated within curriculum materials designed to promote more effective language teaching in special schools (Harris, 1984c). On the other hand 'talking to children', and 'giving them the chance to express themselves' is a much more open-ended activity which bears little resemblance to formal teaching. Objectives are vague, progress is difficult to monitor since its direction is unpredictable and it is almost impossible to associate improvement with specific classroom experiences. The distinction might be summarised as the difference between teaching language-like skills and encouraging language development. It reflects the distinction already made in Chapter Two between intervention strategies which focus on objectives and those which focus on communicative processes.

Because teachers are paid for undertaking a range of professional responsibilities they need to engage in certain activities which validate their professional status. In special schools, teachers need to be seen to be engaged in explicitly pedagogical activities. However, in so far as they are mature individuals with a wide experience of children, the culture in which they grow up and contemporary views about general and linguistic development, they also seem to recognise that language acquisition extends beyond the limited range of skills which can be taught through formal instruction. Further research is therefore needed to clarify the distinction between language instruction and language development within special schools, both in respect of teachers' perceptions and in terms of the specific opportunities which exist for language learning in formal and informal classroom settings.

SUMMARY

This chapter has been concerned with various aspects of classroom practices which focus on language teaching. It is clear that the majority of teachers regard language development as a very important part of their work and make deliberate efforts to introduce their pupils to appropriate learning experiences. The size of the teaching group is a key variable with teachers working with less able children showing a marked preference for small groups and one-to-one teaching while teachers with more able children show a greater use of small groups and 'whole class' activities. In view of the fact that 19 of the 30 teachers working with pre-verbal children cited the use of the Portage System, it also seems likely that in many cases, one-to-one teaching sessions for those less able children are associated with formal and highly structured activities.

Apart from commercially produced programmes, of which Portage was by far the most popular, materials for language activities ranged from toys, picture books and puzzles to technical equipment such as television, video, language masters and micro-computers. The most frequently cited activities for language teaching were looking at picture books, naming activities, singing, drama and physical games.

What is particularly interesting in these descriptions is that they are specifically 'language activities' in which the pupils' use of language, and comprehension of the teachers' language by the pupil, constitutes the lesson objective; the pupils' success and the success of the lesson seem to depend exclusively on the production and comprehension of specific language forms. Furthermore, apart from the rather loosely defined 'games, drama and physical games' those activities seem to equate language with the production and comprehension of referential expressions and ignore other language functions. There is little mention of the child being given the opportunity to ask for information in an appropriate situation, to give instructions or to develop conversational skills. (This is not to say that the children do not experience those learning opportunities in the classroom, only that they do not figure in the teachers' descriptions of planned language activities.)

The descriptions of settings and activities to encourage language learning suggest that the preferred classroom approach involves didactic instruction. The language based activities are very much like any other classroom-based teaching activity found in special schools, except that in the language lesson, the child's speech and appropriate responses to adult speech in themselves constitute the criteria for successful performance. The activities described appear to be based upon the assumption that language learning will take place if referential language relations are demonstrated ('this is a ball - say ball') and by creating the formal conditions in which children's utterances can be made contingent upon certain predetermined perceptual discriminations. In fact, this is hardly surprising considering the extensive clinical and educational literature solely concerned with extending behavioural teaching strategies to the field of language, and the emphasis on behaviourally defined objectives to be found in most language teaching programmes.

It has already been suggested that a triangular relationship between language, action and understanding provides a conceptual basis for describing the language learning experiences of the mentally handicapped child. It may also facilitate the creation of a wider range of classroom activities which are relevant to the young child's acquisition of language. A developmental process approach to language intervention would suggest that the child must first of all be involved in activities which can provide the basis of some form of mental representation or understanding. The development of understanding may itself depend upon the opportunity to communicate with others (Meade, 1934; Vygotsky, 1962; Newson, 1979). The linguistic communication of ideas, that is the ability to express ideas in structurally complex words and sentences, is also dependent upon the language learning child having appropriate social and communicative experiences (Wood, McMahon and Cranstoun, 1980; Tizard and Hughes, 1984). Work on the development of communication among mentally handicapped children may therefore need to focus much more on the kinds of social activity which foster understanding and the communication of personal ideas. Whereas this suggestion appears to represent a considerable departure from the activities described by teachers as central to language learning, it is important to remember that the teachers' comments on 'the single most important thing you can do to encourage the development of language', were much more concerned with children's understanding, and ability to participate in natural discourse.

Thus, the way forward for language teaching in special schools may be to try and resolve the conflict which is created when the notion of instruction (and all the ideological ramifications of education) are counterposed to intuitive ideas about language as a developmental phenomenon. Planned learning experiences and instruction are not indivisible. The planning of learning experiences may also seek to optimise <u>developmental opportunities</u>. In the case of language acquisition, this will involve a theoretical framework derived from research on language acquisition by normal (non-handicapped children) and the design of classroom activities which enhance those processes underlying language. In terms of the triangular relationship already described, this will require a clarification of the ways in which conceptual development creates the conditions for linguistic expression and comprehension, and the ways these two processes are related to the social activities of children and adults. Sufficient research has already been carried out to make this a practically viable and theoretically valid enterprise. This theme is explored in more detail in the final chapter.

Chapter Six

HELP FROM OUTSIDE THE SCHOOLS: THE INVOLVEMENT OF
PROFESSIONALS AND PARENTS

Mentally handicapped children often have a range of
needs which cannot be fully met by the staff
available within the school. These include medical
problems, difficulties with movement, motor
coordination and respiration, specific problems with
learning and social adjustment,and of course speech
and language difficulties. For this reason the
teaching staff in special schools are supported by
representatives from a number of professions who
provide expert advice and, on occasions, specific
therapy for individual children.

In addition to drawing on the services of
members of the health, social and psychological
services, special schools also need to maintain
close contact with the families of their pupils
(Warnock, 1978). One way of doing this is for staff
to visit the homes of pupils in their classes.
However, this is likely to be time-consuming and
therefore impractical except on an intermittent
basis. A more realistic approach might be to
encourage parents to visit schools to see what their
children are doing during the day and to discuss
progress with staff. Close contact between schools
and parents might be expected to have a number of
advantages for the childrens' language development;
it would enable parents and teachers to have an
understanding of how children communicate in
different settings; new abilities which emerged in
one setting could be encouraged in other settings,
and successful ways of working with a child either
at home or at school could be shared, thus
increasing the child's opportunities for learning
and development.

The next section presents the data concerning
the frequency of school visits by professionals and

the kinds of support they provided for language assessment and language teaching. This is followed by a summary of the family background and the data concerned with parental visits and parental involvement in language related activities.

PROFESSIONAL SUPPORT FROM OUTSIDE THE SCHOOL

The majority of the schools were visited with varying degrees of frequency by representatives of different professional groups concerned with education, child health and the social services. Table 6.1 indicates the mean number of half-day visits per week which the heads reported for the different professional groups. It also shows the number of half-day visits by professionals in relation to the number of children in the schools.

Table 6.1: Visits from Members of Other Related Professions

	No. of Half-Day Visits Per Week		No. of Half-Day Visits - No. of Pupils in School	
	Mean Within Schools	Range Within Schools	Mean	Range
Speech Therapist	2.03	0(6)*-7	.05	0-.29
Physiotherapist	2.81	0(6) -8	.08	0-.29
Occupational Therapist	.09	0(30)-2	.002	0-.07
Educational Psychologist	.28	0(23)-1	.006	0-.03
Medical Officer	.41	0(26)-1	.01	0-.09
Researcher	.00	0 -0		
Others	.66	0(20)-5		

* Figures in parentheses indicate the number of schools receiving visits of lower duration and of lower frequency than one half-day per week.

Of all the related professions speech therapists and physiotherapists spent most time in schools. On average schools were visited by physiotherapists for 3 half-days per week, while visits by speech therapists were slightly less frequent averaging about 2 half-days per week. Members of other groups visited on average far less than one day per month. However, some schools fared much better than others in respect of obtaining the services of those professionals. While some schools reported rarely seeing a speech therapist - 'I would like to see a speech therapist at least once per week. We have not seen one for six months. Prior to that it was very spasmodic' - others were receiving seven half-day visits within the school week. Comparisons for average number of visits by speech therapists in the different local authorities indicated substantial variability as is shown by the index of speech therapists' time in relation to the number of pupils in schools (see Tables 6.1 and 3.17). This ranged from .013 in Gwent to .092 in Gwynedd. This index indicates the amount of time the speech therapist has available for each child in the school. Thus, if speech therapists in Gwent wished to see all the children in the school each week and one half-day session involved two hours of contact time with children, they would only be able to see each child for 1 minute 30 seconds. At the other extreme, speech therapists in Gwynedd would be able to see each child for 11 minutes. This is a rough and ready approximation which does not take account of the different needs within the schools, or the different ways in which speech therapists might work. Nevertheless, it does indicate the constraints under which speech therapists operate, and the extent to which those constraints differ between local education authorities.

These data emphasise the relative high frequency of visits by physiotherapists and speech therapists compared with members of other professional groups. They also show considerable variation over different schools with a disturbingly large number of schools reporting seeing representatives of outside professions less than one half-day per week.

Help from Professionals in the Assessment and Teaching of Language and Communication

Of those professionals mentioned by the head as contributing to the assessment or teaching of language and communication in the schools (Table 6.2), speech therapists received by far the most individual mentions, although the majority of heads indicated that members of more than one professional group were involved. Whereas 25 schools were receiving help with the _assessment_ of language and communication, only 16 schools received help with language _teaching_.

Table 6.2: Schools Indicating Help from Related Professions with Assessment and Teaching of Language and Communication

	Assessment	Teaching
Speech Therapist	7	9
Educational Psychologist	2	
Research Worker	1	
Other	1	2
Combination of those listed	14	5
No help	7	16

Total No. of Schools = 32

In the majority of cases assistance from related professionals was either requested by the school or initiated jointly by the staff and the professional concerned. In very few cases did the heads report that the help was provided at the instigation of the professional (see Table 6.3). However, this may be as much a reflection of the tact which those professionals had exercised when initiating assessment and teaching schemes in schools as a true indication of any reluctance to become involved in work in special schools.

Table 6.3: Initial Responsibility for Organising Help by Related Professionals

	Assessment	Teaching
Head and Staff of School	15	7
Professional Concerned	1	3
Both Professional and School Staff	7	5
Other	2	1

Although many teachers carried out language assessments within the classroom, they also had access to a variety of forms of professional help ranging from their classroom aide or nursery nurse to the speech therapists and educational psychologists. Table 6.4 summarises the responses to the question 'Is there anyone other than yourself <u>regularly</u> involved in assessing the communication skills of the children in your class?' This shows that along with speech therapists who assisted 67% of the teachers, the non-teaching classroom staff were the professionals most intimately involved in language assessment. Altogether over 62% of the teachers identified their classroom aide or the nursery nurse as being regularly involved in language assessment. In contrast teachers were seldom involved in language assessment work in classes other than their own. This supports the finding presented earlier that there are relatively few teachers in special schools involved in assisting teachers in classrooms beside their own in working on language and communication.

Table 6.4: Other People Involved in the Assessment of Language and Communication

	Pre-verbal	Single Words	Sentences	Total	%
Non-teaching Class Aide	21	20	14	55	62.5
Other Teachers	4	5	3	12	13.6
Speech Therapist	20	19	20	59	67.0
Educational Psychologist	6	3	7	16	18.0
Others	1	0	2	3	34.0
No-one	2	3	1	6	6.8

LINKS BETWEEN HOME AND SCHOOL

This section presents the questionnaire data in respect of the links between the pupils' parents and the schools. It begins with a brief summary of those aspects of home background which might influence contact between home and school, before considering the extent of parental involvement in the schools.

<u>Residential and Foster Care</u>. Altogether, just over 12% of the pupils in the schools sampled were cared for on a part-time or full-time basis by people

other than their natural or adoptive parents (Table 6.5). These comprised 50 children who lived with foster parents, 78 who were living in residential accommodation for part of each week, and a further 79 children were placed in residential accommodation full-time. The distribution of alternative accommodation varied from school to school. Eleven schools had no children living with foster parents, while in one school there were twelve such children. Similarly, the number of children in full-time residential accommodation varied from zero, in 16 schools, to one school with 18 children.

Table 6.5: Numbers of Children in Foster Homes or in Residential Units

Type of Alternative Provision	N.	Range within Schools	Mean within Schools	% of all Pupils
Pupils in Foster Homes	50	0(11)*-12	1.72	2.9
Pupils in Residential Units				
Full-time	79	0(16)*-18	2.47	4.6
Part-time	78	0(20)*-18	2.44	4.5

* Figures in brackets indicate numbers of schools with no children in each cateogry.

Pupils Experiences of Language Other Than English
Of the total 1,727 pupils 145 (8.4%) came from homes where a language other than English was spoken. Of those, the majority (nearly 90%) came from Welsh speaking homes. Within the schools nineteen of the heads reported that teachers never addressed pupils in the schools in Welsh, six indicated that Welsh was used occasionally in the classrooms, and 7 stated that Welsh was used most of the time. Of the teachers, 25% reported that they regularly addressed one or more children in their class in Welsh.

Participation by Parents
The majority of the heads felt that only a small proportion of parents were involved in helping the children with language and communication and that

the level of parental involvement was insufficient
(Table 6.6). However, when the heads were asked
about the support the school provided for the
parents in this area another aspect of this
situation became apparent. In addition to stating
whether or not they provided parents with help in
relation to teaching language and communication,
those who answered in the affirmative were asked to
describe the help they provided. It was then
possible to sub-divide those schools where help was
provided into those which offered 'active' support
such as special courses, and special parents
evenings and those which offered only 'passive' help
for example, 'open access to school', 'books sent
home', 'diary sent home', 'participation by those
parents who show an interest'. Six heads reported
that they did not provide parents with help. Of the
26 who indicated that they did provide support, 14
provided descriptions which suggested 'active'
support while 12 were categorised as providing
passive help. The overall impression, therefore, is
that only about half of the schools had a deliberate
policy of involving the parents in activities
concerned with language and communication.

Table 6.6: Families Involved in Teaching Language
and Communication

Estimated Extent of Families' Involvement by Headteacher		Heads' Evaluation of Family Involvement	
None	1	Satisfactory	5
Small Number	23		
Many	5	Insufficient	25
Majority	1		
Don't Know	2	No Information	2
	—		—
	32		32

Only five teachers reported having parents come
into the classroom to work with the children
although 41 (47%) said that the results of language
assessments were made available to parents. Parental
participation is a two-way commitment and it seems
likely that the low level of involvement by parents
(Table 3.15) is closely associated with the absence

of parent involvement policies in many of the schools. While it would be over simplistic to suggest that this state of affairs is the product of a simple cause and effect relationship, it may not be unreasonable to suggest that the schools must bear the major responsibility for initiating change.

SUMMARY

This chapter has shown that although the majority of the schools were visited by other professionals including speech therapists, physiotherapists, schools medical officers and educational psychologists, the frequency of visits varied considerably both from school to school and across local authorities. Class teachers received the greatest help in terms of language assessment from speech therapists. Apart from these professionals from outside the school, teachers tended to rely upon their own classroom assistants for help with language assessment. Within the school teachers appear to work as relatively autonomous and isolated professionals with little support from their colleagues. Although some schools were able to cite specific attempts to foster links between home and school, only 47% of teachers routinely made available written language assessments to parents and none mentioned parents as being involved in language assessment. Only five teachers had parents coming into the classroom to work with the children. Thus, not only are the teachers isolated professionally but current classroom practices seem to maintain the dislocation of school and home.

Chapter Seven

SUGGESTIONS BY SCHOOL STAFF FOR IMPROVING PRACTICE

Since one of the objectives of this study was to
describe the ways in which teachers interpreted
their own role in relation to the encouragement of
language development, it was decided to present both
head teachers and class teachers with open-ended
questions about how they felt the assessment and
teaching of language could be most effectively
improved.

THE HEAD TEACHERS

At the end of the questionnaire the heads were asked
to state 'the single most effective way of improving
the language and communication skills of the
children in your school' and finally for any other
comments on the teaching of language and
communication skills in special schools. Specific
suggestions for change or improvements on any aspect
of special educational provision were classified
under several headings (see Table 7.1). A comment
from any head teacher which included more than one
suggestion would be itemised under more than one
heading.

The most frequently stated suggestions referred
to changes in the school curriculum, for example:

Fostering activities that require communication
and have a more practical outcome that gives
satisfaction.

Table 7.1: Heads' Comments on Improving Provision
for Teaching Language and Communication

	No.of Comments Citing each Category
Improved Curriculum	
General Comments	8
Assessment	1
Programmes	3
Computers	1
Improved Social Interactions	
Adult-child (one-to-one)	4
Child to child (groups)	4
Staff Development	
Organisation within School	3
In-service Courses	5
More Staff	3
More Contact With Related Professions	
Speech Therapists	9
Educational Psychologists	1
Adviser	1
Researcher	1
Parental Involvement	
General	2
In-school	1
At home	2
Community Education	1

Encouraging the child to participate in all types of activity, e.g. shopping and visits one day every week, P.E. three times per week and gardening.

To a great extent the value of drama and P.E. in the development of those skills in special school is overlooked. Much emphasis is now being placed on these areas with good results.

Only three comments referred specially to languge programmes, for example:

'An effective language programme'; while one headteacher requested 'more precise assessment' and another urged greater use of computers and video recorders.

The second most frequently mentioned category was additional time from members of related professions and in particular the need for more help from speech therapists:

More sessions from a speech therapist.

In-service sessions for teachers by speech therapist.

Full-time speech therapist (Welsh speaking) as a full-time member of the school staff.

Greater allocation of time for a very good enthusiastic speech therapist to spend more time with pupils and individual staff. One day per week does not positively attack the problem.

It is clear from these comments that although the heads felt that the speech therapists could help, they did not seem to be clear about exactly how they would help. The most clearly expressed statements referred only to speech therapists working with members of staff but did not indicate whether or not the heads had in mind specific skills which ought to be passed on to their staff. This absence of specific comments leaves open the possibility that some heads wished to delegate responsibility for this aspect of the school's work to other professionals who are specifically qualified in the field of language and communication.

The third most frequently cited category was staff development. Some of these comments referred to requests for more staff to provide greater emphasis on language and communication:

Extra staff - using individual work programmes.

Improved pupil/teacher ratio. There needs to be more opportunity for teachers to engage on individual work.

Other comments were concerned with internal re-organisation within the school:

> Probably assigning one member of staff to undertake formal responsibility (for language and communication).

> One person, a teacher, responsible for language and communication programmes throughout the school, reinforced by class teaching daily.

> There must be periods in the timetable given to the subject.

A third group of comments on the theme of staff development referred to in-service training:

> In-service sessions for teachers by speech therapists;

> Thorough in-service training of stafff. This would hopefully achieve two aims: (a) it would provide the intrinsic skills of language development, (b) and would help to change the philosophy of many 'old hands' who regard the emphasis on language and communication work in the curriculum as possibly a threat to established thinking and teaching procedures.

The fourth group of comments were specifically concerned with changes in the types of social interaction experienced by the pupils. These were evenly divided between those which advocated greater emphasis on one-to-one teacher-pupil exchanges:

> important to have as many talking adults around as possible to give the children individual attention;

> by frequent uninterrupted one-to-one sessions for specific problems;

and on the other hand the need for more opportunities for pupil-pupil exchanges:

> Children should be talked to as little as possible (sic) and encouraged to talk to their peer groups and others.

> I have found that placing children who have reached the single or two-word stage amongst other children with good language skills, will improve their skills markedly.

The final area which received comments from a number of heads concerned increased parental involvement:

> Parents need to be involved in language teaching, particularly on non-verbal programmes (Makaton etc.)

> An effective way of bringing paents easily into schools - no cost - so that they can be more involved with teaching methods as well as helping them to realise the importance of talking to their children.

> Something beyond the control of the school. An improvement and emphasis on language and communication in the home. All most of my pupils get from their parents is abuse and comments. They are never read stories and very rarely involved in discussions other than of an aggressive nature.

THE CLASS TEACHERS

In response to a question which asked if there were any changes that teachers would like to introduce in the way they taught language skills, 38 teachers indicated that there were. In response to a follow-up question requesting details of the kinds of changes they would like to see introduced, approximately half referred to changes in the organisation within the school or within their classroom. Some of these changes would require more staff or financial assistance for effective implementaion. The most frequent comments regarding internal changes concerned more time for the teacher to work with children, smaller groups and more opportunities for one-to-one teaching (see Table 7.2). No indication was given regarding the kind of activity which was associated with one-to-one teaching, but it seems likely that it would include structured approaches to teaching specific language skills (see Chapter Four).

Approximately half the comments referred to changes introduced from outside the school. The most frequently cited changes here were language programmes, speech therapy and new approaches and/or information from research. Finally, five teachers, including four who taught children using phrases and sentences, commented on the need for greater opportunities for children to go outside the school so that they had opportunities for using language in natural everyday settings.

These comments suggest dissatisfaction in two distinct but related areas. First, the comments concerned with changes within the school suggest that teachers feel frustrated in terms of the opportunities to carry out the kinds of activity which they regard as being useful for children learning language. The numerous comments regarding individual or small group work illustrates this point. A further example concerns the comments about opportunities for using language in natural settings. These two sets of comments suggest very different views regarding the most appropriate experiences for children learning language, and reflect on the discussion presented earlier concerning a skills approach versus a developmental approach to language intervention. Nevertheless, they both indicate that teachers have clear views about what they would like to do, but that they are prevented from putting those views into practice. In contrast, the other comments regarding different kinds of additional help from outside agencies suggest that many teachers also experience uncertainty in terms of what they ought to be trying to do with the children.

A slightly different question was concerned with the ways in which teachers thought they could be most effectively helped to encourage language and communication skills among mentally handicapped children. They were presented with nine statements describing different kinds of help and asked to rank them in order of helpfulness. The items ranged from suggestions indicating within-school and within-class changes (for example, smaller classes; more classroom assistants) to items which described help and guidance from outside agencies. A summary of the nine statements together with the mean overall ranking is shown in Table 7.3.

Table 7.2: Changes Teachers Would Like to Introduce to the Teaching of Language and Communication (N = 38)

	Pre-verbal	Single Words	Sentences	Total
Changes within the School				
More one-to-one teaching	7	1	4	12
Smaller groups	2	1	0	3
More time	1	0	0	1
Quiet areass/ fewer interruptions	1	0	0	1
Single member of staff responsible for language	1	0	0	1
Additional help from Outside				
Materials/ equipment	1	1	0	2
Language programmes	2	3	2	7
Speech therapy	2	1	2	5
Research information on new approaches	1	3	1	5
Better assessment	0	0	1	1
In-service courses	0	1	0	1
Parental involvement	1	0	0	1
Opportunities for developing children's language in natural settings	1	0	4	5

Suggestions for Improving Practice

Table 7.3 Ranking of Items Concerned with Ways in which Teachers Could be Helped to Encourage Language and Communication (N = 82)

	Overall Mean Rank	Rank Position of Ranks
Smaller classes	4.9	5
More classroom assistants	5.9	8
More equipment	7.2	9
More in-service training courses	4.8	3.5
More opportunity for discussion of individual children with professionals	3.6	2
More co-operation from parents	5.0	6
More information on what other teachers do	4.8	3.5
Sensible suggestions from experts	3.0	1
A wider selection of structured language teaching programmes	5.6	7

Kendall's Coefficient of Concordance, $W = .2041$, $df = 8$, $p \leqslant 0.001$

The data were examined for agreement between teachers regarding the pattern of rankings using Kendall's coefficient of Concordance (Siegel, 1956). This produced a W of .2041 (n = 82, df 8, $p \leqslant .0001$) which suggests a very high degree of agreement between teachers. The item regarded as being the most helpful was 'sensible suggestions from experts for practical classroom activities which would assist the development of language'. This was closely followed by 'more opportunity to discuss individual children with other professionals such as speech therapists and educational psychologists'. The high ranking of those two items suggests a need for recommendations about what teachers can do. However, this did not extend to all kinds of help. 'A wider selection of structured language

programmes' for example, was ranked consistently low
with a mean overall rank of 5.6, as was more co-
operation from parents (mean rank 5.0). On the other
hand, 'greater provision for in-service training
courses' and 'more information about what other
teachers with similar children do to encourage
language skills', were both rated as being
comparatively helpful suggestions.

In contrast to suggestions concerned with
specific activities, items describing within-school
and within-classroom organisational changes, were
rated as being less helpful. For example, smaller
classes attained a mean rank of 4.9, more classroom
assistants a mean rank of 5.9 and more equipment a
mean rank of 7.2. These data indicate that the most
pressing problem for most teachers is having a clear
idea of suitable activities which will be beneficial
for language acquisition. Within-school and within-
class changes in materials, staffing levels and
class size seem to be considered generally as being
of less importance.

SUMMARY

For both head teachers and class teachers, the
invitation to comment on possible improvements in
the school's approach to language and communication
produced a wide range of suggestions. Both groups
emphasised, on the one hand, within-school changes
concerned with the language curriculum and
organisational aspects of the classroom and on the
other hand, the need for more support from
professionals from outside the school. These two
types of comment may be interpreted in different
ways. First, it is possible that the staff have
clear ideas about what is needed within the school,
but regard additional expert help as essential to
introducing appropriate innovations. The second
interpretation suggests that the two types of
comment actually reflect different perceptions of
desirable changes. Whereas some staff have a clear
idea of what they feel would constitute improved
practice, and therefore see outside help as being of
less importance, others are, in fact, much less sure
and would seek advice and guidance from
professionals outside the school. This second
interpretation is supported by the final rating
scale item in which the class teachers were asked to
rank, in order of priority, nine suggestions for
improving work on language and communication within

the classroom. The most popular items proved to be concerned with 'suggestions from experts for practical classroom activities' and the opportunity to discuss individual children with experts. Both of these items indicate some concern among teachers regarding appropriate classroom activities for encouraging language and communication. In contrast, changes within the classroom concerning class size, available class help and equipment were ranked lowest. These data together point to considerble uncertainty and concern among teachers regarding exactly what <u>are</u> appropriate classroom activities for promoting language and communication among mentally handicapped children.

Chapter Eight

SUMMARY AND DISCUSSION: CURRENT PRACTICE AND FUTURE PROSPECTS

This study has attempted to provide an initial overview of the educational practices concerned with language teaching in special schools within the eight local authorites in Wales. Comparable information for all areas of language assessment and teaching with respect to special schools in England, Scotland and Northern Ireland is not as yet available. However, where comparable data does exist this has been mentioned. Much of the report has been concerned with different aspects of staffing, school organisation, teaching methods and teachers' views on educational practices. This summary is an attempt to bring together many of these findings under broad thematic headings, to indicate possible interpretations of these data and to suggest practical implications.

The research was conceived within a theoretical framework which emphasises the cognitive and social characteristics of developmental change. Social cognition provides a theoretical perspective which sees ordinary children changing over time in respect of behaviours and abilities including language and suggests that it is necessary to credit children with some kind of underlying knowledge or representations of real world events in order to account for the speed and complexity of some of these visible developmental changes. Furthermore, it emphasises that progressive developmental outcomes are the result of continuous interactions between the child and the social and physical environment. Of particular importance are the social processes which underly developmental change. It has been suggested that it is the meanings which are made available to children as a result of participation in communicative interactions with others which

118

enables them to organise and interpret experience in a social way and hence to become social beings.

Since language is essentially a social activity it follows that social interactions available to a child will influence the speed and course of language development. In the special school, the opportunities available to the child for learning through interaction will depend partly upon the physical environment, but more importantly, upon the way in which the adult caretakers interpret their role within the school, and the extent to which organisational and ideological factors promote or inhibit facilitative social interactions.

The question of language assessment is also directly tied to theoretical considerations. Linguistic theory has expanded to include a rich and complex set of descriptive tools for the analysis of child language. Assessments employed in schools will be influenced by a host of factors including the extent to which staff are aware of the different levels of linguistic description (grammatical, semantic, pragmatic) the availability of instruments which incorporate these different theoretical perspectives and the extent to which the staff themselves value different kinds of linguistic ability for the pupils with whom they work.

Since so much depends upon the teaching skills, and their theoretical perspectives it makes sense to begin this final chapter with a review of the teachers' background qualifications, and their contact with other professionals.

THE TEACHERS

The heads reported that some 80% of teachers possessed initial teacher training qualifications while of the 88 teachers who completed questionnaires nearly 90% had initial teacher training qualifications. Only three teachers had PGCE qualifications, the rest holding either Bachelor in Education or Certificate in Education qualifications. Only 55% of the teachers were qualified within the field of special education or the education of children with handicapping disorders and less than 20% had attended in-service courses concerned with language and communication during the preceding year. In view of the expectation that mentally handicapped children (those with severe learning difficulties) should receive educational provision in relation to their special needs (Warnock, 1978) a very large number of teachers in this study seemed to lack either appropriate basic training or recent experience of specialised in-service courses.

However, before suggesting that more in-service courses are necessary it is necessary to consider the structure of teacher training in Britain for teachers working in schools for children with severe learning difficulties. In 1984 Sir Keith Joseph recommended the closure of initial training courses catering specifically for students going into special education. Instead all teachers would be trained for primary or secondary employment and would only move into special education after experience of working with ordinary children (D.E.S. Circular 3/84 Welsh Office Circular 21/84). The rationale for this decision was apparently based upon an elision of the two meanings of special education; special education represented not only the special needs of certain pupils, but also the specialist skills of teachers. Just as doctors and social workers had adopted a model of a broad based generic training and practical experience prior to specialisation, so teachers would need to embrace the same career structure in respect of special education.

At the time few politicians and educational administrators questioned the wisdom of this decision or the extent to which the skills and methods appropriate to the ordinary primary and secondary school were appropriate to schools for severely mentally handicapped pupils. In retrospect, and in view of the data presented in this report, there are good reasons to believe that a generic training is not in itself sufficient as a basis for curriculum planning and implementation in the special school.

In particular teachers in special schools need far greater understanding of the course of early development and the contribution made by different kinds of experience. Although 80% of the teachers possessed an initial teacher training qualification 'sensible suggestions from experts' was the form of additional help seen as most desirable. This suggests that whatever the merits of initial courses, they are not meeting the perceived needs of the teachers themselves in relation to language and communication.

Finally, the very low figure relating to recent attendance in in-service courses about language and communication, invites further clarification. Is the low attendance because of apathy among the teachers, the limited availability of relevant courses or the level of support provided by the local authorities and the head teachers in making time available during the school day for attendance on such courses? It might seem that the prospects of curriculum innovation in this area are very bleak so long as the present system of initial training and the low attendance of staff in in-service courses continues.

A more optimistic view might be that schools can and do initiate their own forms of in-service training and that staff can learn from each other and from the other professionals who come to the school. However, there was little evidence of specialist help or guidance being available from within the schools. Only 14 of the 32 schools represented in the heads' responses, had a designated teacher with special responsibility for the teaching of language and communication. Of these only 2 worked with other members of staff, while the rest worked directly with the children, either in groups or individually. Of the teachers who filled in questionnaires, just over 10% reported that they had special responsibility for language and communication with respect to children in other classes and about the same number had similar responsibilities for signing. Approximately 53% stated that classroom based assessments of childrens language were made available to other teachers, but only 13% reported that other teachers were actually involved in helping to produce these assessments. This suggests that many teachers receive relatively little help and support from their colleagues.

OTHER STAFF

Approximately 87% of the teachers reported that they had at least one non-teaching classroom assistant, nursery nurse, or teacher's aide. Provision of auxiliary staff varied considerably across schools, with some schools having one non-teaching member of staff for every three children while in other schools, the ratio was as low as 1:25. Although auxiliary staff have been referred to here as non-teaching to differentiate them from qualified teachers, it is clear that very often they were intimately involved in educational activities with the children. For example 62% of the teachers indicated that the auxiliary staff were actively involved in making written assessments of language and communication abilities and 81% of teachers stated that written language assessments were normally made available to their non-teaching assistants. The way in which teachers used their non-teaching assistants within the classroom, and in particular their involvement in social and communicative activities with the children, is an area which deserves a more detailed consideration than was possible within the scope of this study.

AVAILABILITY OF PROFESSIONAL AND PARENTAL HELP FROM OUTSIDE THE SCHOOLS

Because of the wide range of psychological, physiological and medical problems experienced by pupils in special schools, the staff normally have access to a wide range of specialists. However, the frequency with which different professionals visited the schools varied considerably. Overall, speech therapists were the professionals who spent most time in special schools, but their availability fluctuated across schools; some schools saw a speech therapist for less than one half day per week, while staff in other schools reported having speech therapists in attendance for 7 half days in a 5 day week. This variation was not accounted for by variations in the size of the school populations.

A high proportion of teachers (67%) reported that speech therapists were actively involved in guiding assessments of language and communicative abilities and 75% reported classroom based assessments were made available to other professionals including speech therapists. Whereas 25 heads reported that their schools were receiving help from speech therapists in relation to the assessment of pupils' language and communication, only 16 reported that speech therapists were actively engaged in teaching or advising teachers on forms of language intervention within the classroom. Both head teachers and class teachers indicated that they would like to have more frequent visits from speech therapists and, when asked to rank the importance of various sources of possible help, teachers placed 'more opportunities to discuss individual children with experts' second overall.

These data indicate a very uneven distribution of professional services to special schools. This was evident even when these and other resources were examined in relation to size of school. Secondly, it

underlines the view that most teachers in special
schools receive relatively little help from
professionals outside the school, and even less from
their teacher colleagues. Teaching language and
communication in special schools appears to be a
relatively isolated activity in which teachers must
depend very much on their own resources to develop
interesting and worthwhile activities for the
children and to guide their classroom assistants.

What is not clear from this study is the way in
which head teachers and class teachers perceive the
role of experts or the way in which experts present
themselves when visiting schools. Among the
questions which need to be answered are, what kind
of advice the professionals are able to offer to
teachers, to what extent the teachers are able to
feel part of a professional team when working with
other professionals, and to what extent visiting
professionals are involved in staff training and
development. A fundamental issue concerns the extent
to which visiting professionals are able to extend
and develop staff competencies and how far they are
seen as individuals who will themselves assume
responsibilities for certain areas and thus absolve
the staff from the need for either decision making
or independent action.

In about half of the schools there was little
indication of a positive attempt to involve parents
in language related activities with their children
and only 5 teachers reported parental participation
within the classroom. Over 70% of the head teachers
felt that the level of parental involvement within
the school was 'insufficient'. Just as teachers
received little help from other professionals, so
they seem to be doing relatively little to actively
encourage parental participation either at school or
while the children are at home. Obviously there are
many reasons why there is so little direct contact
with parents including limited time and, in some
cases, the unwillingness of parents to co-operate.
However, it is also likely that the teachers'
position within the organisation of the special
school contribute to these difficulties. Without
substantial support from colleagues and other
professionals they may lack the motivation and the
skills necessary for developing positive and
productive relations with parents. With this in mind
it is suggested that fostering links between home
and school ought to be given greater emphasis by
head teachers and by local authority advisers. It
should also be possible to arrange in-service

training courses which deal directly with this issue.

THE PUPILS

The majority of the 1727 children included in this study were described by teachers as either mentally handicapped or multiply handicapped, with mental handicap being but one of their disabling characteristics. However, both head teachers and class teachers reported some anomalous children who were identified as suffering from only sensory impairment, or only presenting behaviour problems. The ages of all children varied considerably from as low as 24 months to 21 years. The age range of children within a class diminished in relation to the ability range of the class: classes with pre-verbal children had the widest age range, and classes with children using sentences had the narrowest age range. Similarly, there were relatively more children who were described as multiply handicapped in the pre-verbal classes and relatively more children who were described as mentally handicapped (but without additional problems) in the classes where children were using phrases and sentences.

The number of children for whom each teacher was responsible varied from as few as 4 to as many as 11. However, this variation balanced out within schools so that whether one looks at overall figures of staff and pupils from the heads' questionnaire or the number of children taught by class teachers who filled in the teachers' questionnaires, the mean teacher pupil ratio was approximately 1:8. It is likely that teachers with similar classes were also in charge of more difficult or demanding children, and that those with larger classes were concerned with more able and socially responsive children. However, this is only conjecture and the study did not seek to examine in detail the differences between children in large classes and children in smaller classes.

The children in a school represent the focus for the educational practices adopted, so the characteristics of those children will determine to what extent different kinds of activities are judged desirable and practicable. The number of pupils within a class and the extent to which their needs and abilities are seen as disparate and requiring individual attention rather than group activities, will also place constraints on classroom organisation and the possibilities for introducing different learning experiences. The size of classes, both within and between schools, and the basis for grouping pupils into teaching groups is an area closely related to curriculum design, and presumably to the procedures adopted for language assessment and language teaching. While it would be premature to make recommendations on the basis of the data presented in this study, these results emphasise the importance of recognising the organisational and practical difficulties associated with the implementation of new ideas.

ASSESSING LANGUAGE

A rating scale was employed to examine what teachers saw as the main goals of language assessment. When they were asked to place statements describing the purpose of language assessment in rank order, the most popular items proved to be concerned with planning teaching objectives, understanding the child and monitoring progress. This result emphasises the implications of language development becoming established as a subject for instruction within the context of a lesson. The primary purposes of assessment are perceived as being to establish what is to be taught - that is the <u>content</u> of the lesson, and to ascertain retrospectively, how effective teaching has been in establishing specific new behaviours. In this way the assessment procedure enables the teacher to expropriate language from the child, so that it can become the legitimate subject of a lesson. Assessment as a source of information for communication with other professionals was ranked relatively low in order of priority and the least popular item concerned assessing the effectiveness of teaching. This emphasises both the teachers' isolation within the school, and suggests a reluctance to perceive language development as part of an ongoing social process in which the teacher bears equal responsibility with the child for successful communication.

Written assessments of children's linguistic or communicative abilities were made relatively infrequently; just over half the teachers (58%) reported making written assessments once per term, while about 22% did so more frequently, and 20% less frequently. These assessments were made available to head teachers, classroom assistants and other

125

professionals (most frequently speech therapists). About half the teachers reported making their language assessments available to other teachers, and about the same number made assessments available to parents. It should however, be pointed out that no further questions were asked about when and why such assessments were made available, and to what extent availability resulted in other teachers and parents reading or acting upon those assessments.

Although 44% of teachers described assessment procedures used in addition to formal tests and charts, most teachers used at least one of these instruments either 'frequently' or 'sometimes'. The most frequently cited procedures were general indices of developmental progress, which included some items specifically concerned with language and communication (e.g. Portage Scheme, Gunzberg P.A.C. Charts). Reliance upon these procedures suggests that language was not being assessed in very much depth or breadth by teachers within the classroom.

One likely reason why the Portage checklist was so popular as an assessment instrument is that it forms part of a more general teaching programme. The programme involves descriptions of behaviour in various domains (language, self help, socialisation etc.) organised into a putative developmental sequence. Assessment involves identifying the child's level of ability in respect of this sequence, and then selecting the next behaviour in the sequence as a teaching objective. The recommended teaching methods involve typical behavioural procedures such as reinforcement and shaping. Employment of this programme therefore suggests a traditional 'skills' approach to language development work and promotes the view that language is a set of behaviours which can be taught (for a more detailed discussion of these views see Harris, 1984a;1986).

It might also be that the popularity of the Portage checklist and the Gunzberg Progress Assessment Charts is related to the simple direct language which is used to describe linguistic and communicative abilities and their ease of use for teachers working in busy classrooms.

Finally, it might be assumed that the availability and use of a practical assessment instrument by teachers will interact with teachers' views on child language. While they are unlikely to use an instrument which is impractical and difficult to understand or which is inconsistent with their existing views on language, it is also likely that whenever a commercially available form of assessment is employed it will tend to confirm the theoretical perspectives on which it is based for those who use it. Similarly, if teachers can be encouraged to use assessment instruments which reflect a broad theoretical base and address grammatical, semantic and pragmatic aspects of language, this is likely to extend and enrich their understanding of the scope and complextity of child language.

LANGUAGE TEACHING

Responses to the questionnaire items concerned with language teaching provided additional evidence of a highly structured approach within the schools and classrooms involved in this study. Of the 32 head teachers, 16 reported that they required their staff to indicate on a timetable specific periods when they would be undertaking language work, and 84% of the teachers reported that they did in fact set aside specific periods for language related activities.

Thus for many teachers attempts to encourage language development were, within the organisational framework of the schools, accorded the status of lessons. However, lessons are not traditionally concerned with cognitive development, so much as the transmission of knowledge from one individual to a group of others (Jones and Williamson, 1979; Kohlberg and Mayer, 1972). Sixty-six per cent of the teachers who set aside specific lesson periods for language activities indicated that they usually worked with individual children, while only 20% reported that they usually worked with the whole class. The emphasis upon one-to-one teaching was even more noticeable with teachers who worked with pre-verbal children; 88% of these teachers reported a preference for working with individual children. Here again there is an emphasis upon language as a skill which must be taught individually under conditions within which the teacher has maximum control of both the lesson content and the teaching process.

Of the 32 schools included in the study, 31 reported using a sign or symbol system of some kind; 29 schools used Makaton and of these, in 19 schools, Makaton was the only system being used. Sixty-two per cent of teachers had at some time been on a course concerned with signing or use of a symbol system. Makaton was by far the most widely used

127

system among teachers with 67% using it with at least one child in their class. These results are very similar to those reported by Jones, Reid and Kiernan (1982). Of the non-signing language schemes, 42% of teachers reported using the Portage Scheme while the next most popular scheme was Jim's People, being employed by 15% of the teachers.

Both of these schemes focus on breaking language down into discrete graded objectives and using behavioural principles to encourage the child to produce specific verbal responses following appropriate cues. In doing so they make it relatively easy for the teacher to incorporate 'language' as a subject within the school curriculum. However, such approaches receive little support from recent theories of language development (Harris, 1984a).

In addition to the commercially available schemes, teachers used a variety of other materials when focussing on language teaching. Among the most commonly cited materials were picture books, toys and puzzles. Descriptions of teaching activities included looking at pictures and picture books, singing and playing 'whole body' games (particularly with the pre-verbal children) and naming activities in respect of pictures, objects and actions. There appeared to be very little in terms of any formal or consciously expressed theory of language development or language teaching guiding these activities. In the majority of cases teaching activities seemed to be guided by the idea that language learning depends upon passive participation (for example, imitation and rehearsal) and that the meanings of words could be learned through repetition of target words within a physical context which, in the teacher's view, defined an appropriate referent. Some teachers gave descriptions of linguistic categories (for example names, action words, pronouns, propositions) as the target of their language work but there were very few occasions in which the objectives in terms of such linguistic descriptions were closely related to a set of procedures for achieving specific objectives. Needless to say, it is impossible to determine to what extent this reflects the actual planning and conduct of language related activities and to what extend it is an artefact of the use of a postal questionnaire. It does however suggest that this is an area which deserves further detailed study.

When teachers were asked about the single most important thing they could do to encourage language and communication skills many of them produced descriptions which focussed upon spontaneous, natural and conversational uses of language in contrast to the structured settings and elicited target utterances which characterised descriptions of _actual_ classroom teaching. It is suggested that this divergence reflects the ways in which many of the teachers have responded to the contradictory pressures of wishing to encourage 'natural' language and also having to tackle language as a curriculum subject within an organisational and administrative framework which emphasises individual instruction and behaviourally defined objectives. A solution to the dilemma produced by placing language development on the list of curriculum subjects for special schools is suggested below.

SUGGESTIONS BY SCHOOL STAFF FOR IMPROVING PRACTICE

Various suggestions were made by both class teachers and head teachers for improving the quality of pupils' language learning experiences. These could be divided into those that focussed on within-school or within-class changes and those that were concerned with help from outside the school. It is suggested that the within-school changes are a reflection of teachers having relatively clear ideas about how teaching for language and communication should be arranged, while suggestions for changes from outside the school indicate greater uncertainty and an awareness of the need for clear guidelines for useful classroom activities. When asked to rank in order of importance nine specific suggestions for improving work on language and communication, the teachers involved in this study consistently gave priority to sources of help from outside the school. If the quality of education provided for severely mentally handicapped pupils in special schools is to be improved, greater efforts must be made to provide teachers with additional professional support and training. Furthermore, within-school staff training and organisational changes to encourage individual teachers to develop expertise and take responsibility for specific curriculum and or developmental areas would seem to be highly desirable. In this way schools themselves might become more effective in recognising and meeting the professional needs of their various staff members.

THEORY AND PRACTICE IN LANGUAGE TEACHING

It has been suggested that the ways in which teachers appear to be conceptualising their language teaching activities runs parallel to recent trends within developmental psychology about the kind of description which is necessary to characterise language learning among non-handicapped children. A traditional distinction has been between competence and performance; that is to say a child's knowledge of language as opposed to the language he or she actually produces (Chomsky, 1968). More recently, cognitive psychologists have become interested in the range of competencies which appear to be necessary for ordinary language use; knowledge underlying language use is not assumed to be merely concerned with grammatical or phonological rules (Slobin, 1973), but with the way in which the physical world can be understood, (for example, Edwards, 1973) and the ways in which pre-verbal and verbal social interactions are organised and co-ordinated (Bates, 1976; Bruner, 1983). Alongside this interest in the child's personal knowledge of language, there has also arisen a concern with the way in which the social environment provides a context which both sustains social and linguistic interactions and creates processes whereby actions and words can be endowed with meaning (Nelson, 1985). Although the expressed views of teachers are seldom complete in respect of descriptions of psychological processes, individual linguistic skills and the social context, it is suggested that teachers' existing intuitive knowledge may provide the basis for the elaboration of a more complete and sophisticated theoretical framework which could then be used to guide language teaching and language assessment. More specifically, it should be possible to provide a theoretical description of language teaching which makes explicit and practically relevant the relationship between:

1) The activities in which adults engage children when they are focussing on language: that is to say, in schools, the way in which teachers structure the social and physical context for language use and language leearning.
2) The expectations the teacher has for the child's communicative and linguistic performance in that setting.

3) The child's knowledge of language, social interactions and the physical world which may reasonably be expected to underly that peformance.

4) The extent to which such knowledge may be expected to facilitate the occurrence of similar communicative and or linguistic behaviours in other social and physical settings.

Such an approach has the advantage of being theoretically consistent with contemporary research concerned with language development among normal children without being constrained by developmentally sequenced language curriculae (see Chapter Two). It avoids the trap of equating language with verbal behaviour and of assuming that the aim of language intervention is to teach mentally handicapped children to use the same structures, meanings and functions which researchers have described in the language of ordinary children at different ages. This approach has the additional advantages of being highly flexible and yet closely related to existing classroom practices and contemporary methods of linguistic analysis.

A New Approach to Language Teaching in Special Schools

One of the ways in which this style of language facilitation might be achieved is through the application of recent research on event knowledge (Schrank and Abelson, 1977). Nelson (1985) and her colleagues suggest that young children organise their understanding of common experiences in terms of a general event representation (GER). Experiences are understood in terms of specific contexts, the roles adopted by people within those contexts and the actions performed by the children themselves. Frequently occurring activities which have a specific purpose, clearly defined roles for the participants and a set of materials or props which are regularly employed, may become particularly well established in the child's mind. The mental representations of such events are referred to by Nelson as scripts. For young children script knowledge is likely to develop in relation to such activities as getting dressed, eating lunch or going to buy something in a shop. For example, the script for buying something from a corner sweet shop might include the roles of customer and shopkeeper and the props might be money, weighing scales, paper bags and sweets. The goal of buying sweets would be achieved through the participation of the role holders (the child and the shopkeeper) in specific sub-script routines. For example:

Main Script	Sweet Shop
Roles	Customer - Shopkeeper
Goal	To obtain sweets
Subscript 1	Entering: move into shop
	look for favourite sweets
Subscript 2	Buying: wait for turn
	indicate which sweets and how many
Subscript 3	Paying: wait for indication of cost
	hand over money
	wait for change
Subscript 4	Exiting: take sweets
	check change
	leave by door

While the list of sub-scripts and the event details may resemble a functional analysis or a skills breakdown of a complex skill within the behavioural tradition, the underlying theory of event knowledge is very different. To begin with, whereas the behavioural functional analysis is a description of a task in preparation for teaching, a script is intended to be a description of an individual's knowledge of a situation. Nelson suggests that script knowledge expands over time and becomes more elaborate as the child gains more experience of different contexts. Thus, it is by participation in those activities which are organised sequentially over time that the child attains a better understanding of the script. Furthermore, since scripts are an example of general event representation, they have a high degree of commonality across experiences. Thus, a sweet-shop script developed in one shop, will be applicable to other corner sweet shops, and to other shops selling different items. The script would be less applicable in a supermarket where the sub-scripts tend to be substantially different, but it would still provide a general event structure within which suitable sub-scripts could be elaborated.

Just as Nelson has argued that event representation is made possible by the child's repeated involvement in social routines which share a common underlying structure, so Bruner has suggested that the pre-verbal child learns about the process of communication through repeated involvement in social activities which have a predictable structure (Bruner, 1983). For example, the game of peek a boo provides a child with possibilities for social interaction with another person. At first the infant may be relatively passive and only respond to events after they have occurred - for example, after the mother places a napkin or towel over the infants face it is pulled away. Subsequently, the infant may anticipate such actions and place the napkin over his or her own face. Later on the infant may instigate the game and take on the role of agent who covers the mother's face with the napkin. Bruner argues that such social activities enable the child to make sense of experience precisely because the adult maintains a clear structure and interprets the child's activity in the light of that structure. This in turn provides the child with the possibility of making sense of his/her own behaviour within the constraints of the game structure. From such simple repetitive games Bruner argues that children develop ideas about turn-taking and intentional comm-unciation.

In the case of language learning, Nelson and her colleagues suggest that the representation of social routines enables adult and child to agree on what it is that will be talked about. The events and their associated mental representations provide a common context for adult and child through which the meanings expressed in language are mutually interpretable by the participants. It therefore facilitates the child's attempts to understand the meanings of the adult's utterances and, similarly, provides a framework within which the adult can interpret the child's words and reflect the inferred meaning back to the child.

Nelson and her colleagues describe three ways in which event contexts (that is routines for which adult and child have mental representations) can support the child's attempts at linguistic communication. First, shared event knowledge facilitates conversation between adults and young children. Secondly, as routines become established in event representations, it is argued that the child needs to focus less attention on understanding the routine and working out the part he or she has to play. This in turn, means that the child has more time to think about expressing ideas through language.

Summary and Discussion

A third way in which shared event knowledge may increase the child's language is by enabling the adult to play a more effective part in maintaining conversational exchanges. Bruner (1983) and Nelson et al. (1985) propose four specific strategies which enable adults to support the child's participation in dialogue. First, 'scaffolding' is the process by which the adult provides the general structure of a conversation and leaves the child to fill in gaps which are carefully manufactured to match the child's linguistic ability. Secondly, adults selectively extend the scope of the situations within which specific utterances can be used and the functions they can perform. Thirdly, adults enable the child to extend their communicative abilities without risk of losing their way; in Bruner's terms they provide a 'communicative ratchet' which limits the consequences of any misunderstandings which may arise when children attempt to use new words or novel constructions. Finally, adults can exploit their understanding of a child's non-linguistic knowledge within the context of a social routine, so that they can deliberately increase the chances of the child seeking to communicate aspects of that knowledge.

The views of Bruner and Nelson indicate that for children to make sense of the world around them they need to be involved in social routines which have a clear structure and which facilitate communicative interactions between the child and his caretakers/teachers. This argument was based on work with non-handicapped infants and young children. However, the implications for work with mentally handicapped children are clear.

A child who faces a world that is constantly changing, that does not provide the kind of repeatable event structure that makes a stable event representation possible, cannot achieve this kind of stability. We call this the chaos factor and stipulate that it may have broad repercussions for impairment of cognitive functioning when stable representations are not established and thus do not become available for cognitive processing (Nelson, 1985, p. 247).

These ideas suggest specific strategies for the design of language intervention in special schools. Instead of focussing on language as a curriculum subject, teachers might seek to develop social

134

routines which could provide the basis of event representations. Indeed, the special school day is replete with the kinds of activity which could be exploited in this way. Extra-curricular activities such as arriving and leaving school, mid-morning breaks for drinks, and lunch times, all provide appropriate settings for the elaboration of social routines. In terms of classroom activities, research already exists to show the potential of activities such as doll play (e.g. bed-time or a tea-party) and 'cooking' with playdough for stimulating language (Brinker, 1982; Harris, 1984b).

Participation by adults and mentally handicapped children in such routines might be expected to facilitate conversation, increase the child's cognitive resources which can be deployed for communication and enable adults to employ effective support strategies. Such activities would differ in a number of important respects from traditional teaching activities. While the activities could be developed to encourage language and communication, language would not be the subject of the lesson in the traditional sense. The activities would be designed and elaborated to create the conditions within which language and communication could flourish.

Secondly, although routines might be established with teachers working with individual pupils, they would be equally well suited to working with groups of children (Harris, 1984b). Thirdly, it is not possible to identify in advance the specific language forms or the functional characteristics of the language which might occur. Social routines are regarded as attempts to facilitate those processes which are implemented in language development; the precise nature of the linguistic outcomes will only be identifiable retrospectively. Finally, it is suggested that this approach offers a way not only of encouraging language, but also of establishing those social and cognitive abilities which are precursors to language and upon which langue development is founded.

SUMMARY

A social routine with a high degree of structure is referred to by Nelson <u>et al</u>. as a script. Participation in such routines is likely to lead to the development and elaboration of general event representations. This is both a significant

135

cognitive achievement, and the cognitive basis for the emergence of language. It is suggested that the characterisation of school based activities in terms of scripts provides the first step towards engaging mentally handicapped children in the kinds of social interactions which will facilitate communication and language. Because the script is both a characterisation of real life events and an attempt to describe mental representations it offers a particularly promising approach to language intervention. At one level the script is a description of what a child understands about a routine, but at another more concrete level, it describes the appropriate actions and related language of the people who adopt the script roles. For this reason it seems to present a highly practical approach to the design of classroom activities for promoting language development.

Appendix 1

HEAD TEACHERS' QUESTIONNAIRE

LANGUAGE AND COMMUNICATION IN SPECIAL SCHOOLS

QUESTIONNAIRE FOR TEACHERS

SECTION ONE - TO BE COMPLETED BY HEAD TEACHER

1. How many children are currently attending your
    school as full time pupils? ☐

2. What categories of handicap are included among
    the children in the school?
    (Please tick appropriate box for each item)

    i. mental handicap only (including delayed
       development and slow learners)

       majority of the children ☐

       some children ☐

       only 1 - 2 children ☐

       none ☐

    ii. physical handicap only (including epilepsy
        and cerebral palsy)

        majority of the children ☐

        some children ☐

        only 1 - 2 children ☐

        none ☐

    iii. sensory handicap only (i.e. blind/partial
         sight; deaf/partial hearing)

         majority of the children ☐

         some children ☐

         only 1 - 2 children ☐

         none ☐

iv. behaviour problem <u>only</u> (including maladjustment)

majority of the children

some children

only 1 - 2 children

v. mental handicap <u>plus</u> at least one other handicap (sensory handicap, physical handicap, behaviour problem)

majority of the children

some children

only 1 - 2 children

3a. What is the age of the oldest child in the school?

yrs   mths

3b. What is the age of the youngest child in the school?

yrs   mths

4a. How many children over the age of 16 years are there in the school?

4b. How many children under the age of 5 years are there in the school?

5. How many classes are there in the school?

6. Are the children placed in teaching groups according to:-

	yes	no
Age		
Development		
Mobility		
Social adjustment		
Language and communication skills		

Other - please specify _____

7a. How many children in your school come from homes where a language other than English is normally spoken?

7b. How many children come from Welsh speaking homes?

8. How many teachers are there on the staff?

9. How many teachers have an initial teaching qualification? (Cert.Ed., B.Ed., P.G.C.E., etc.)

10. How many of the teachers have a qualification in the following areas?

    i. children with special educational needs

    ii. the education of mentally handicapped children or slow learners

    iii. the education of children
        with other forms of
        handicap (e.g. blind
        children, deaf children,
        physically handicapped
        children)

11. Have any teachers attended a course
concerned with the assessment and teaching
of language and communication skills
(including sign language) during the past
year?

        yes ☐ no ☐

If 'YES' what was the course and how many
teachers attended?

   i. Course title _____

  ii. Duration _____

 iii. Organised by _____

  iv. Held at _____

   v. Was there an award or qualification upon
     satisfactory completion of the course?

        yes ☐ no ☐

     If 'YES' what organisation was responible
     for making the award?

     _____

  vi. How many teachers from your school
     attended the course? ☐

12. Is there any member of the teaching staff with
a special responsibility for organising
language and communication work throughout the
school?

        yes ☐ no ☐

If 'YES' does this teacher normally work directly with individual children, or with groups of children from classes other than his/her own class?

individual children [　　　]   groups of children [　　　]

13. How many classroom staff other than teachers are there in your school?

   i. Nursery nurses

  ii. Teaching assistants

 iii. Teaching aides

  iv. Other - please specify _____

14. How many of these other members of staff have a qualification in education or child care?

[　　　]

15. Have any of the other members of staff been on a course concerned with the assessment and teaching of language and communication skills during the last year?

yes [　　] no [　　]

If 'YES' what was the course and how many staff other than teachers attended?

   i. Course title _____

  ii. Duration _____

 iii. Organised by _____

  iv. Held at _____

v. Was there an award or qualification upon satisfactory completion of the course?

yes ☐ no ☐

If 'YES' what organisation was responsible for making the award?

_____

vi. How many staff other than teachers attended? ☐

16. Please indicate how much time on average the following specialists spend working with teachers and pupils in your school?

Number of <u>half days</u> per week

	Morning					Afternoon				
Speech Therapist	1	2	3	4	5	1	2	3	4	5
Physiotherapist	1	2	3	4	5	1	2	3	4	5
Occupational Therapist	1	2	3	4	5	1	2	3	4	5
Educational Psychologist	1	2	3	4	5	1	2	3	4	5
School Medical Officer	1	2	3	4	5	1	2	3	4	5
Research Workers	1	2	3	4	5	1	2	3	4	5
Others - please specify	1	2	3	4	5	1	2	3	4	5

_____

17. Do you and your staff receive any help from people outside the school in <u>assessing</u> the language and communication skills of your pupils?

yes ☐ no ☐

If 'YES' please answer questions 17(b), 17(c) and 17(d).

If 'NO' please go to question 18.

17(b) Please give a brief description of the help provided.

_____

_____

_____

_____

17(c) Who provides help?

    i.   Speech Therapist

    ii. Educational Psychologist

    iii. Research Worker

    iv. Other - please specify

_____

17(d) Who was initially responsible for organising this?

    i.   You (Head teacher)

    ii. The staff

    iii. The specialist concerned

    iv. Someone else - please specify

_____

18. Do you and your staff receive any help from
     experts outside the school regarding the
     <u>teaching</u> of language and communication skills
     to your pupils?

     yes [   ] no [   ]

     If 'YES' please answer questions 18(b), 18(c)
     and 18(d).

     If 'NO' please go on to question 19.

     18(b) Please give a brief description of the
            help you have received.

     _____

     _____

     _____

     _____

     18(c) Who provided the help?

            i.   Speech Therapist

            ii.   Educational Psychologist

            iii. Research Worker

            vi.   Other - please specify

     _____

     18(d) Who was initially responsible for
            arranging this help?

            i.   You (Head teacher)

            ii.   Other member(s) of staff

            iii. The specialist concerned

            vi.   Other - please specify

     _____

19. When not in school, how many of the children are cared for in:

    (a) Foster homes

    (b) Residential units of hospitals

         (i) all of the time

         (ii) at least part of each week

20. How many parents/guardians take an active part in teaching language and communication skills when the children are at home?

    i.   None

    ii.   A small number of parents

    iii. Many of the parents

    iv.   The majority of parents

    v.   All of the parents

    vi.   Don't know

21. How do you regard the level of parental involvement in teaching language and communication skills to the children in your school?

    i.   Excessive

    ii.   Satisfactory

    iii. Insufficient

    iv.   No information

145

22. Does the school provide help for parents in terms of how they can encourage language development and communication while their child is at home?

   yes ☐ no ☐

   If 'YES' please describe the help which is provided.

   _____

   _____

   _____

   _____

23. Is a Sign Language or Symbol System used in the school?

   yes ☐ no ☐

   If 'YES' what system is used?

   i.   Makaton vocabulary ☐

   ii. Paget Gorman Sign Language ☐

   iii. Blissymbolics ☐

   iv. American Sign Language (AMSLAN) ☐

   v.   British Sign Language (BSL) ☐

   vi. A system devised by you or one of our colleagues ☐

   vii. Other - please specify

   _____

24. How many teachers in your school are able to use sign language?

   ☐

25. How often is the Welsh language used in the classroom?

    Never

    Seldom

    Most of the time

26. Do you require your staff to indicate on the timetable specific periods during the week when they will be teaching language and communication skills?

    yes ☐ no ☐

27. (a) At what time do the children normally arrive at school?

    _____

    (b) At what time do the children normally leave school at the end of the day?

    _____

    (c) How long is the lunch break? Hrs Mins

    ☐ ☐

28. What do you feel would be the single most effective way of improving the language and communication skills of the children in your school?

    _____

    _____

    _____

    _____

29. Do you have any other comment on the teaching
    of language and communication skills in
    special schools?

    _____

    _____

    _____

    _____

Thank you very much for your generous help. A
Stamped Addressed Envelope is provided to assist you
in returning the completed questionnaire.

Appendix 2

CLASS TEACHERS' QUESTIONNAIRE

LANGUAGE AND COMMUNICATION IN SPECIAL SCHOOLS

QUESTIONNAIRE FOR TEACHERS

* SECTION THREE - TO BE COMPLETED BY A TEACHER WHO
WORKS WITH CHILDREN WHO USE MAINLY SINGLE WORDS
(EITHER SPOKEN LANGUAGE OR SIGNS).

(*Sections two, three and four are identical in
content, but are addressed to teachers working with
children of different levels of linguistic ability).

1.   How many children are there currently in your
     class? ☐

2.   How many children in your class fall into the
     following categories:

     i.   mentally handicapped only
          (including developmental   ☐
          delay and slow learners)

     ii. physically handicapped only
          (including epilepsy and   ☐
          cerebral palsy)

     iii. sensory handicap only
          (i.e. blind/partial sight;   ☐
          deaf/partial hearing)

     iv. behaviour problems only   ☐
          (including maladjustment)

     v.   mental handicap plus at least
          one other handicap (sensory   ☐
          handicap, physical handicap,
          behaviour problem)

3a. What is the age of the oldest child in your
     class?
                              yrs   mths
                              ☐   ☐

3b. What is the age of the youngest child your class?

yrs   mths

4. How many of the children in your class come from Welsh speaking homes?

5. How often do you normally make a written assessment of the language and communication skills of the children in your class?
(Please tick one box)

    i.   seldom if at all

    ii.   about once a year

    iii. about once a term

    iv.   at least once per week

6a. When you make a written assessment of a child's language ability, is this for your own use or is it normally made available to other people?

    i.   own use

    ii. made available to others

6b. If it is made available to other people, who would normally see your assessment?
(Please tick the appropriate boxes)

                                    yes   no

    i.   your assistant,
          teacher's aide,
          nursery nurse etc.

    ii.   other teachers on
          the staff

    iii. your head teacher

iv. the child's parents $\square$ $\square$

v. other professionals
(e.g. speech
therapist,
educational
psychologist) $\square$ $\square$

vi. local authority
advisers $\square$ $\square$

vii. others - please specify

_____

7. When assessing language and communication
skills do you use any of the charts and tests
listed below?
(Please tick appropriate box for each item)

	freq-uently	some-times	never
i. Sheridan Scales			
ii. Derbyshire Language Scheme			
iii. Reynell Language Scale			
iv. Hester Adrian Language Charts			
v. Language Charts from 'Let Me Speak'			
vi. Gunzberg Progress Assessment Charts			
vii. Portage Checklist			
viii. National Children's Bureau Developmental Guide			
ix. Teacher's Developmental Assessment Charts			

    x. L.A.R.S.P.

   xi. D.I.S.T.A.R.

  xii. Others - please specify

_____

8. Are there any other methods which you would normally use to monitor the language and communication skills of the children in your class?

                          yes [ ] no [ ]

If 'YES' please give a brief description

_____

_____

_____

_____

9. Is there anyone other than yourself <u>regularly</u> involved in assessing the language abilities of the children in your class?
(Please tick the appropriate box for each item)

                                    yes   no

    i. nursery nurse

   ii. teacher's aide/
       teaching assistant

  iii. another teacher

   iv. speech therapist

    v. educational
       psychologist

   vi. other - please specify

_____

152

10. What do you regard as the main purpose of assessing the language abilities of the children in your class?
(Please indicate how important you regard the following alternatives by numbering them from 1 to 5. Place a figure 1 in the box against the item which you regard as the most important aim of assessment; place a figure 2 in the box against the item which you regard as being next in order of importance and so on until you have numbered all the boxes.)

to provide the teacher with information so that he/she can talk knowledgeably about the child to other teachers, professionals and parents ☐

to enable the teacher to monitor the child's progress ☐

to help the teacher to assess the effectiveness of teaching ☐

to provide a basis for planning relevant teaching objectives ☐

to help the teacher to understand the child better ☐

11. Among all the activities which you undertake with the children in your class during the week, how important do you regard the development of language abilities?
(Please tick the description which best fits your views).

Very important   Of some importance
☐   ☐

Not very important Of no importance
☐   ☐

12. Do you set aside particular periods during the week for teaching language skills?

yes ☐ no ☐

If 'YES' please answer questions 12(b) to 12(e)

If 'NO' please go to question 13.

12(b) Briefly describe the sorts of activity you would normally include in periods devoted to encouraging language development - it may help to focus on the things you do with one specific child

_____

_____

_____

_____

12(c) When working on language skills do you work with:
(Please tick appropriate boxes)

	usually	some-times	hardly ever
i. the whole class together			
ii. small groups of children			
iii. individual children			

12 (d)   What materials and equipment do you
         reqularly use when teaching language
         skills?
         (Please tick appropriate box for each
         item)

                                        yes   no

         i. toys (if yes please
            give examples)

         _____

         ii. picture books

         iii. puzzles

         iv. television/
             video-recorder

         v. audio-tape recorder

         vi. language master

         vii. micro-computer

         viii. other - please specify

         _____

12 (e)   About how much time do you normally
         spend working specifically on
         language skills?

                                        hrs   mins

         i. Approximate amount of
            time per day

         ii. Approximate amount of
             time per week

Class Teachers' Questionnaire

13. Are you teaching any of the children in your
    class to use sign language or a symbols
    system?

    yes ☐   no ☐

    If 'YES' please indicate which of the following
    most accurately describes the system(s) you are
    using.

    i.   Makaton Vocabulary

    ii.   Paget Gorman Sign Language

    iii. Blissymbolics

    iv.   American Sign Language
          (AMSLAN)

    v.   British Sign Language
          (BSL)

    vi.   A system devised by you or
          one of your colleagues

    vii. Other - please specify

    _____

14. Do you regularly use any language kits or
    teaching programmes when working on language
    development with the children in your class?
    (Please tick the appropriate response for
    each item)

                                    yes   no

    i.   Portage

    ii.   Let Me Speak

    iii. Gillham's First Words
          Programme

    iv.   Derbyshire Language
          Scheme

    v.   L.A.R.S.P.

vi.   D.I.S.T.A.R.

vii.   Jim's People

viii. Other - please specify

_____

15. Apart from teaching periods specifically
     devoted to encouraging language and
     communication skills, how much opportunity
     do the children in your class have for
     practising language skills during the school
     day?
     (Please tick the description which best
     describes your view)

     No opportunity   Very little opportunity

     Some opportunity   Numerous opportunities

16. What do you feel is the single most important
     thing you can do to encourage the development
     of language and communication skills in the
     children you work with?

     _____

     _____

     _____

     _____

157

17. Are there any changes you would like to make in
    the way you teach language skills?

    yes ☐ no ☐

    If 'YES' please describe the changes you would
    most like to introduce.

    _____

    _____

    _____

    _____

18. Below are a number of statements describing the
    role of the teacher in the development of
    language and communication. Please indicate how
    far you agree or disagree with each statement.
    (Please tick the appropriate box for each
    statement)

    The teacher is the most important single
    influence on the mentally handicapped child's
    progress in learning to communicate.

    Strongly agree Agree Disagree Strongly disagree
    ☐   ☐   ☐   ☐

    Providing the child is not too severely
    handicapped communication and language will
    develop irrespective of what the teacher may
    do.

    Strongly agree Agree Disagree Strongly disagree
    ☐   ☐   ☐   ☐

    The child's parents are in a better position to
    influence language development than the
    teacher.

    Strongly agree Agree Disagree Strongly disagree
    ☐   ☐   ☐   ☐

Encouraging mentally handicapped children to develop language is a highly skilled job.

Strongly agree Agree Disagree Strongly disagree

Once a child is mentally handicapped, the teacher is really wasting his/her time in trying to teach language.

Strongly agree Agree Disagree Strongly disagree

19. Below are a number of statements expressing different views on the development of language and communication amongst mentally handicapped children. Please indicate how far you agree or disagree with each statements. (Please tick the appropriate box for each statement)

A child must understand the meaning of at least some words before he can communicate

Strongly agree Agree Disagree Strongly disagree

It is important that adults always try and respond to a child's attempts to communicate even when it is difficult to understand exactly what the child is saying.

Strongly agree Agree Disagree Strongly disagree

When working with a child who is only using one word at a time the teacher's most important task is to get the child to use phrases and simple sentences.

Strongly agree Agree Disagree Strongly disagree

It is very important that mentally handicapped children are taught to speak clearly right from the start.

Strongly agree Agree Disagree Strongly disagree

159

Handicapped children can usually express a great deal more than they put into words.

Strongly agree Agree Disagree Strongly disagree

☐ ☐ ☐ ☐

Teaching a child to use signs or symbols will discourage him/her from using spoken language.

Strongly agree Agree Disagree Strongly disagree

☐ ☐ ☐ ☐

Teaching mentally handicapped children to read is a good way of encouraging language development.

Strongly agree Agree Disagree Strongly disagree

☐ ☐ ☐ ☐

20. How do you think teachers such as yourself can best be helped to encourage the development of language and communication skills amongst mentally handicapped children?
(Please indicate how important you regard the following alternatives by numbering them from 1 to 9. Place a figure 1 in the box against the suggestion you regard as most helpful; place a figure 2 against the suggestion you regard as next most helpful and so on until you have numbered all the boxes).

Smaller classes ☐

More classroom assistants ☐

More equipment (please give examples) ☐

Greater provision for in-service training courses for teachers ☐

More opportunities to discuss individual children with other professionals such as speech therapists and educational psychologists ☐

More co-operation from parents ☐

More information about what other
teachers with similar children
do to encourage language skills

Sensible suggestions from experts
for practical classroom activities
which would assist the development
of language

A wider selection of structured
language teaching programmes

21. Do you have special responsibility for teaching
    language to children in <u>other</u> classes?

    yes [ ] no [ ]

22. Do you have special responsibility for teaching
    signing or a symbol system to children in
    <u>other</u> classes?

    yes [ ] no [ ]

23. How much help do you have in your class?

    No help [ ]

    Nursery nurse(s)

    Number full time [ ]   Number part time [ ]

    Teaching assistants(s)

    Number full time [ ]   Number part time [ ]

    People supported by a Government training
    scheme (e.g. Y.O.Ps., M.S.C., Y.T.S.)

    Number full time [ ]   Number part time [ ]

Class Teachers' Questionnaire

Parents

Number full time ☐   Number part time ☐

School children

Number full time ☐   Number part time ☐

24. How long have you spent working with mentally handicapped children (E.S.N.S?)
(If you have had extended periods away in other jobs or having a family, simply discount the time away and indicate the total number of years overall in which you have been employed in an E.S.N.S. school or in a junior training centre).
(Please tick one box)

0 - 2 years ☐

2 - 5 years ☐

5 - 10 years ☐

10 - 15 years ☐

15 - 20 years ☐

20 years or more ☐

25. Do you have an initial teaching qualification?

yes ☐   no ☐

If 'YES' please specify which qualification.

Teaching Certificate ☐   B.Ed. ☐   P.G.C.E. ☐

Instructor ☐   Instructor Q.T.S. ☐

Date of award _____

26. Do you have a special qualification in one of the following areas?

	yes	no
i. children with special educational needs	☐	☐
ii. the education of mentally handicapped children	☐	☐
iii. the education of children with other forms of handicap (e.g. blind children, deaf children, physically handicapped children)	☐	☐

If 'YES' please state

i. name of qualification _____

ii. awarding body _____

iii. whether this involved part-time or full-time study

PT ☐   FT ☐

iv. period of study:

	month	year
start	☐	☐
finish	☐	☐

27. Have you been on a course in the <u>last year</u> concerned with the assessment and teaching of communication and language skills to mentally handicapped children?

yes ☐ no ☐

If 'YES' please provide further details:

Title of course _____

Where the course was held _____

How long did the course last _____

Was there an award or qualification upon satisfactory completion of the course?

yes ☐ no ☐

If 'YES' what organisation was responsible for making the award?

_____

28. Have you <u>ever</u> attended a course on using sign language or a symbol system with mentally handicapped children?

yes ☐ no ☐

If 'YES' please give further details:

What sign/symbol system was taught _____

When did you attend the course _____

Where was the course held _____

How long did the course last _____

Was there an award or qualification upon satisfactory completion of the course?

yes ☐ no ☐

If 'YES' what organisation was responsible for making the award?

_____

29. Are the children you normally teach classified as 'special care' children?

yes ☐ no ☐

30. How many of the children in your class do you usually address in Welsh? ☐

31. Please indicate whether you are male or female.

M ☐ F ☐

32. Do you have any additional comments?

_____

_____

_____

Thank you very much for your generous help. A Stamped Addressed Envelope is provided to assist you in returning the completed questionnaire.

BIBLIOGRAPHY

Bailey, P. and Jenkinson, J. (1982) The application of Blissymbols, in P. M. Peter and R. Barnes (eds.) Signs, Symbols and Schools. Stratford: National Council for Special Education.

Bates, E. (1976) Language and Context: the Acquisition of Pragmatics. New York: Academic Press.

Berry, I. (1978) Teachers Developmental Assessment Charts. Liverpool: Alder Hey Hospital.

Blank, M., Gessner, M. and Esposito, A. (1979) Language without communication. A case study. Journal of Child Language, 6, 329-352.

Bloom, L. (1970) Language Development: Form and Function in Emerging Grammars. Cambridge, Massachusetts: M.I.T. Press.

Bloomfield, L. (1933) Language. New York: Henry Holt (reprinted 1961).

Bohannon, J. N. and Marquis, A. L. (1977) Children's control of adult speech. Child Development, 483, 1002-8.

Bowerman, M. (1976) Semantic factors in the acquisition of rules for word use and sentence construction, in D. M. Morehead and A. E. Morehead (eds) Normal and Deficient Child Language. Baltimore: University Park Press.

Braine, M. D. (1963) The ontogeny of English phrase structure: the first phrase. Language, 39, 1-14.

Braine, M. D. (1976) Children's first word combinations. Monographs of the Society for Research in Child Development, 41, 1, 164.

Brinker, R. P. (1982) Contextual contours and the development of language, in M. Beveridge (ed.) Children Thinking Through Language. London: Edward Arnold.

Broen, A. (1972) The verbal environment of the language learning child. American Speech and Hearing Association Monographs, No. 17.

Brown, R. (1973) A First Language. Cambridge, Massachusetts: Harvard University Press.

Bruner, J. (1975) The ontogenesis of speech acts. Journal of Child Language, 2, 1-19.

Bruner, J. S. (1983) Child's Talk. Oxford: Oxford University Press.

Chesaldine, S. and McConkey, R. (1979) Parental speech to young Down's Syndrome children: an intervention study. American Journal of Mental Deficiency, 83, 612-620.

Chomsky (1968) Language and the mind. Reprinted in A. Bar-Adon and W. F. Leopold (eds) Child Language: A Book of Readings. New Jersey: Prentice Hall, 1971.

Clark, E.V. (1983) Meanings and concepts, in P. H. Mussen (ed.) Handbook of Child Psychology. Vol. 3. New York: John Wiley.

Cross, T. G. (1977) Mothers' speech adjustments: the contribution of selected child listener variables, in C. E. Snow and C. A. Ferguson (eds) Talking to Children: Language Input and Acquisition. Cambridge: Cambridge University Press.

Cross, T. G. (1978) Mother speech and its association with rate of linguistic development in young children, in R. Waterson and C. Snow (eds) The Development of Communication. London: John Wiley.

Crystal, D. (1979) Working with LARSP. London: Edward Arnold.

Crystal, D., Fletcher, P. and Garman, M. (1976) The Grammatical Analysis of Language Disability. London: Edward Arnold.

Cunningham, C. C. and Jeffree, D. J. (1971) Working with Parents. Manchester: National Society for Mentally Handicapped Children.

Department of Education and Science (1984) Circular No. 3/84. London: H.M.S.O.

De Paulo, B. M., Bellam, A. and Bonvillian, J. D. (1978) The effect on language development of the special characteristics of speech addressed to children. Journal of Psycholinguistic Research, 7, 189-211.

Dore, J. (1976) Childrens illocutionary acts, in R. Freedle (ed.) Discourse Relations: Comprehension and Production. LEA: Hillsdale NJ.

Dore, J. (1978) Conditions for the acquisition of speech acts, in I. Markova (ed.) The Social Context of Language. Chichester: John Wiley.

Edwards, D. (1973) Sensory motor intelligence and semantic relations in early child grammar. Cognition, 2, 395-434.

Elliot, A. J. (1981) Child Language, Cambridge: Cambridge University Press.

Fillmore, C. J. (1968) The case for case, in E. Bach and R. T. Harms (eds) Universals in Linguistic Theory. London: Holt, Rinehart and Winston.

Fraser, C., Bellugi, U. and Brown, R. (1973) Control of grammar in imitation, comprehension and production, in C. A. Ferguson and D. I. Slobin (eds) Studies of Child Language Development. New York: Holt Rinehart and Winston.

Gibbs, T. (1982) Language assessment of ESN(S) children. Special Education Forward Trends, 9, 1, 23-26.

Guess, D., Sailor, W. and Baer, D. M. (1974) To teach language to retarded children, in R. E. Schiefelbusch and L. L. Lloyd (eds) Language Perspectives: Acquisition, Retardation and Intervention. Baltimore: University Park Press.

Gunzberg, H. C. (1973) Progress Assessment Charts. London: National Association for Mental Health.

Halliday, M. A. K. (1975) Learning How to Mean: Explorations in the Development of Language. London: Edward Arnold.

Harris, J. (1984a) Teaching children to develop language: the impossible dream? in D. J. Muller (ed.) Remediating Children's Language: Behavioural and Naturalistic Approaches. London: Croom Helm.

Harris, J. (1984b) Encouraging linguistic interactions between severely mentally handicapped children and teachers in special schools. Special Education Forward Trends, 11, 2, 17-24.

Harris, J. (1984c) Early language intervention programmes: an update. Association of Child Psychology and Psychiatry Newsletter, 6, 2.

Harris, J. (1985) The limits of psychological intervention in special schools. Early Child Development and Care, 20, 1, 49-66.

Harris, J. (1986) The contribution of developmental psychology to the education of mentally handicapped children in special schools, in J. Harris (ed.) Child Psychology in Action. London: Croom Helm.

Harris, J. (forthcoming). Language - Development Implications for Clinical and Educational Practice. London: Methuen.

Hawkins, P. (1984) Introducing Phonology. London: Hutchinson.

Hinde, R. A. (1986) Causes of Development from the Perspective of an Integrated Developmental Science. Paper presented at the British Psychological Society/E.S.R.C. Conference 'Causes of Development'. University of Stirling, June 1986.

Jeffree, D. and McConkey, R. (1976) Let Me Speak. London: Souvenir Press.

Jones, L. M., Reid, B. D. and Kiernan, C. C. (1982) Signs and symbols: the 1980 survey, in M. Peter and R. Barnes (eds) Signs, Symbols and Schools. Stratford: National Council for Special Education.

Jones, K. and Williamson, J. (1979) Birth of the school room. Ideology and Consciousness, 6, 59-110.

Kiernan, C. (1982) Communication, signs and symbols, in M. Peter and R. Barnes (eds) Signs, Symbols and Schools. Stratford: National Council for Special Education.

Kiernan, C. (1984) Review of language teaching programmes, in D. Muller (ed.) Remediating Children's Language: Behavioural and Naturalistic Approaches. London: Croom Helm.

Knowles, W. and Masidlover, M. (1982) Derbyshire Language Scheme. Unpublished - limited availability through Derbyshire County Council.

Kohlberg, L. and Mayer, R. (1972) Development as the aim of education. Harvard Educational Review, 42, 4, 449-98.

Kyle, J. and Woll, B. (1982) British Sign Language, in M. Peter and R. Barnes (eds) Signs, Symbols and Schools. Stratford: National Council for Special Education.

Leeming, K., Swann, W., Coupe, J and Mittler, P. (1979) Teaching Language and Communication to the Mentally Handicapped. Schools Council Curriculum Bulletin No. 8. London: Evans/Methuen.

Lock, A. (ed.) (1978) Action, Gesture and Symbol: The Emergence of Language. London: Academic Press.

Lock, A. (1980) Language development, past, present and future. Bulletin of the British Psychology Society, 33, 5-8.

Markova, I. (1986) Causes and Reasons in Social Development. Paper presented at the British Psychological Society/E.S.R.C. Conference 'Causes of Development'. University of Stirling, June 1984.

MacNamara, J. (1972) Cognitive basis of language learning in infants. Psychological Review, 74, 1-13.

McTear, M. (1985) Children's Conversation. Oxford: Blackwell.

Meade, G. H. (1934) Mind, Self and Society. Chicago: University of Chicago Press.

Mercer, N. and Edwards, D. (1981) Ground rules for mutual understanding: a social psychological approach to classroom knowledge, in N. Mercer (ed.) Language in School and Community. London: Edward Arnold.

Miller, J. F. and Yoder, D. E. (1974) An ontogenetic language teaching strategy for teaching retarded children, in R. E. Schiefelbusch and L. L. Lloyd (eds) Language Perspectives: acquisition, retardation and intervention. Baltimore: University Park Press.

Musselwhite, C. R. and St. Louis, K. W. (1982) Communication Programming for the Severely Handicapped. San Diego: College Hill Press.

National Children's Bureau Developmental Guide: 0-5 Years. (Experimental version, 1977). London: National Children's Bureau.

Nelson, K. (1973) Structure and strategy in learning to talk. Monographs of the Society for Research in Child Development, 38, 1-2, No. 149.

Nelson, K. (ed.)(1985) Event Representation and Cognitive Development. Chicago: Lawrence Erlbaum Associates.

Nelson, K. E. (1977) Facilitating children's syntax acquisition. Developmental Psychology, 13, 2, 101-107.

Newson, J. (1979) Intentional behaviour in the young infant, in D. Shaffer and J. Dunn (eds) The First Year of Life: Psychological and Medical Implications of Early Experiences. Chichester: Wiley.

Newson, J. and Newson, E. (1973) Intersubjectivity and the transmission of culture: on the social origins of symbolic functioning. Bulletin of the British Psychological Society, 28, 437-46.

Ochs, E. (1979) Introduction: what child language can contribute to pragmatics, in E. Ochs and B. Schieffelin (eds) Developmental Pragmatics. New York: Academic Press.

Ochs, E. and Schieffelin, B. (eds)(1979) Developmental Pragmatics. New York: Academic Press.

Ochs, E. and Schieffelin, B. (eds.) (1983) Acquiring Conversational Competence. London: Routledge and Kegan Paul.

Piaget, J. (1970) Piaget's Theory, in P. H. Mussen (ed.) Carmichael's Manual of Child Psychology, 3rd edn. New York: Wiley.

Rees, M. L. (1978) Pragmatics of language acquisition, in R. L. Schiefelbusch (ed.) Bases of Language Intervention. Baltimore: University Park Press.

Reynell, J. (1969) The Reynell Developmental Language Scales. London: N.F.E.R.

Romaine, S. (1984) The Language of Children and Adolescents. Oxford: Blackwell.

Rowe, J. (1982) The Paget-Gorman Sign System, in M. Peter and R. Barnes (eds) Signs, Symbols and Schools. Stratford: National Council for Special Education.

Ryan, J. (1973) When is an apparent deficit a real deficit? Language assessment in the subnormal, in P. Mittler (ed.) Assessment for Learning in the Mentally Handicapped. Study Group Number 5. Edinburgh: Churchill Livingstone.

Ryan, J. (1974) Early language development, in M. P. M. Richards (ed.) The Integration of a Child into a Social World. Cambridge: Cambridge University Press.

Ruder, K. (1978) Planning and programming for language intervention, in R. L. Schiefelbusch (ed.) Bases of Language Intervention. Baltimore: University Park Press.

Schaffer, R. (1971) The Growth of Sociability. Harmondsworth: Penguin.

Schaffer, R. (1977) Turn-taking, in H. R. Schaffer (ed.) Studies in Mother-Infant Intervention. London: Academic Press.

Schrank, R. and Abelson, R. (1977) Scripts, Plans, Goals and Understanding. Hillsdale, NJ: Lawrence Erlbaum Associates.

Scollon, R. (1979) A real early stage: an unzippered condensation of a dissertation on child language, in E. Ochs and B. Schieffelin (eds) Developmental Pragmatics. New York: Academic Press.

Searle, J. (1969) Speech Acts: An Essay in the Philosophy of Language. Cambridge: Cambridge University Press.

Shearer, D. E. and Shearer, M. S. (1976) The Portage Project: a model for early childhood intervention, in T. J. Tjossem (ed.) Intervention Strategies for High Risk Infants and Young Children. Baltimore: University Park Press.

Sheridan, M. D. (1973) Children's Developmental Progress, 2nd Edn. Windsor: N.F.E.R.

Shotter, J. (1975) Images of Man in Psychological Research. London: Methuen.

Bibliography

Siegel, S. (1956) Non Parametric Statistics for the Behavioural Sciences. Tokyo: McGraw Hill.

Skinner, B. F. (1957) Verbal Behaviour. New York: Appleton-Century Crofts.

Slobin, D. I. (1973) Cognitive prerequisites for the acquisition of grammar, in C. A. Ferguson and D. I. Slobin (eds) Studies of Child Language Development. New York: Holt, Rinehart and Winston.

Snow, C. E. and Ferguson, C. A. (eds)(1977) Talking to Children: Language Input and Acquisition. Cambridge: Cambridge University Press.

Stern (1977) The First Relationship: Infant and Mother. London: Open Books.

The Education Authorities Directory and Annual (1983) Redhill: The School Government Publishing Company.

Thomas, B., Gaskin, S. and Herriot, P. (1978) Jim's People, 2nd edn. St. Albans, Herts: Hart-Davis Educational.

Tizard, B. and Hughes, M. (1984) Young Children Learning. London: Fontana.

Tomlinson, S. (1981) Educational Subnormality: A Study in Decision Making. London: Routledge and Kegan Paul.

Van Oosterom, J. (1982) Rebus at Rees Thomas School, in M. Peter and R. Barnes (eds) Signs, Symbols and Schools. Stratford: National Council for Special Education.

Vygotsky, L. S. (1962) Thought and Language. Cambridge, Mass: M.I.T. Press.

Walker, M. and Armfield, A. (1982) What is the Makaton Vocabulary? in M. Peter and R. Barnes (eds) Signs, Symbols and Schools. Stratford: National Council for Special Education.

Walkerdine, V. (1982) From context to text: a psychosemiotic approach to abstract thought, in M. Beveridge (ed.) Children Thinking Through Language. London: Edward Arnold.

Warnock, M. (1978) Committee of Inquiry into Children with Special Educational Needs. London: H.M.S.O.

Wells, G. (1979) Influences of the Home on Language Development. Paper given to the SERC and SCRE Seminar on Language in the Home. Cardiff, January, 1979.

Welsh Office (1984) Circular No. 21/84. London: H.M.S.O.

Wood, D., McMahon, L. and Cranstoun, Y. (1980) Working with Under Fives. London: Grant McIntyre.

AUTHOR INDEX

Author Index

SUBJECT INDEX

Bliss symbolics 42-3
  use in schools 67-8, 71

Class sizes 47

Gunzberg Progress Assessment Charts 76

Jim's People 84, 128

Language Assessment
  advanced and delayed language 15-6
  appropriate and inappropriate language 15
  criteria for comparisons 14-5
  descriptions of child language 17-23
  in schools
    availability 75-6, 126
    frequency 73, 75, 125
    methods used 76-8, 79, 127
    purpose 72-3, 125
  Methods of assessment 23-7
    developmental scales and charts 25-6
    formal and informal methods 23-4
    language profiles 26-7
    standardised tests 25
Language Curriculum 4-6, 40-1
  (see also management of innovation)
Language Development
  comprehension and production 17
  functional approaches 20-1
  general event representation 131-2
  semantic approaches 19-20
  simplified linguistic input 33-4
  social and cognitive prerequisites 31-3
  social context of interactions 34-7, 131-6
  structural approaches 18-9
  theoretical perspective 5-7, 118-9
Language Teaching
  activities 128-9
  adult child interaction 132-5
  and language development 99
  behavioural approach 27-9
  developmental training 30-1

175

LIVERPOOL POLYTECHNIC
I. M. MARSH CAMPUS LIBRARY
BARKHILL ROAD, LIVERPOOL,
L17 6BD   051 724 2321 ext. 216